FEB    2014

ISSUES THAT CONCERN YOU

# Underage Drinking

Lauri S. Scherer, *Book Editor*

**GREENHAVEN PRESS**

*A part of Gale, Cengage Learning*

GALE
CENGAGE Learning·

Detroit • New York • San Francisco • New Haven, Conn • Waterville, Maine • London

Elizabeth Des Chenes, *Director, Publishing Solutions*

*For more information, contact:*
Greenhaven Press
27500 Drake Rd.
Farmington Hills, MI 48331-3535
Or you can visit our Internet site at gale.cengage.com

For product information and technology assistance, contact us at

Gale Customer Support, 1-800-877-4253
For permission to use material from this text or product, submit all requests online at www.cengage.com/permissions

Further permissions questions can be e-mailed to permissionrequest@cengage.com

Articles in Greenhaven Press anthologies are often edited for length to meet page requirements. In addition, original titles of these works are changed to clearly present the main thesis and to explicitly indicate the author's opinion. Every effort is made to ensure that Greenhaven Press accurately reflects the original intent of the authors. Every effort has been made to trace the owners of copyrighted material.

Cover image © Piotr Marcinski/Shutterstock.com.

**LIBRARY OF CONGRESS CATALOGING-IN-PUBLICATION DATA**

Underage drinking / Lauri S. Scherer, book editor.
   p. cm. -- (Issues that concern you)
 Includes bibliographical references and index.
 ISBN 978-0-7377-6300-3 (hbk.)
1. Teenagers--Alcohol use--United States. 2. Youth--Alcohol use--United States.
3. Drinking age--United States. I. Scherer, Lauri S.
  HV5135.U4222 2012
  362.2920835'0973--dc23
                                      2012029202

Printed in the United States of America
1 2 3 4 5 6 7 16 15 14 13 12

# CONTENTS

In April 2012 the *Los Angeles Times* reported that dozens of teens were ending up in emergency rooms after getting drunk on hand sanitizer. High school students took the alcohol-based germ killer, added salt to separate out the alcohol, and drank what liquid remained. Because the alcohol was so concentrated (and the product not intended for human consumption), the teens developed life-threatening alcohol poisoning. "It is kind of scary that they go to that extent to get a shot of essentially hard liquor,"[1] said Cyrus Rangan, director of the toxicology bureau for the county public health department and a medical toxicology consultant for Children's Hospital Los Angeles. "First thought here: Gross," wrote *Christian Science Monitor* reporter Stephanie Hayes. "Second: Wow. Really sad."[2]

Hand sanitizer is the latest, but not the first, household product teens have turned to in lieu of being able to buy alcohol legally. Certain kinds of cold and cough medicines, oral hygiene products (like mouthwash), and cooking ingredients, like baking extracts, have been treated as replacement beer in teens' unending, cross-generational quest to imbibe. Indeed, limited by a drinking age of twenty-one, teens have come up with a plethora of reckless, odd, and dangerous ways to get a buzz. Some, for example, have participated in the growing trend of soaking tampons in vodka and inserting them vaginally or rectally. Similar to "butt chugging" (where teens insert one end of a tube into their rectum and force alcohol into it), teens who try this are seeking a quick buzz and a way to fool a breathalyzer test. One teen describes the trouble her friend got into after inserting a vodka-soaked tampon in herself:

> She was falling down drunk. The school called the cops and her parents. When the cops came, they gave her a breathalyzer, and she passed! So then they took her to the hospital because they thought that she had done drugs. They had to do a blood test to figure it out, and then she finally confessed

that she had put the tampon in. She was so embarrassed. . . . They say that when you put it in, it goes right into your bloodstream. So you get drunk really fast. Plus, you don't smell like alcohol since you didn't drink it, and you can pass the breathalyzer. Even the boys do it.[3]

When teens go to these extremes to experience alcohol, adults are forced to ask themselves: What is the true effect of withholding alcohol from teens? Does it protect them from abusing alcohol or put them in greater danger by enticing them to try anything for a buzz?

For some, trends like drinking hand sanitizer and soaking tampons in vodka are proof that young people are not mature enough to handle alcohol, and that if anything, it should be harder to get, not easier. Joanne Glasser, president of Bradley University in Peoria, Illinois, points this out when discussing the death of a nineteen-year-old student at her university who died when his drunk friends accidently set his room on fire. "I do not believe for a moment that Bradley's tragedy would have been avoided had alcohol been easier to get," said Glasser, who also pointed out that alcohol played a role in the death of a twenty-two-year-old student, who stumbled into traffic while drunk. "Clearly the fact that [this student, who was of legal drinking age,] could access alcohol legally did not protect him from misusing it,"[4] she said. "When alcohol becomes more readily accessible to young people, alcohol-related problems . . . go up,"[5] agrees *Consumer Affairs* correspondent Sara Huffman. The solution for Glasser, Huffman, and others is therefore less alcohol, not more.

Yet John McCardell could not disagree more. He is the founder of the Amethyst Initiative, a collection of college chancellors and presidents who think lowering the drinking age to eighteen is a good first step to reducing the critical problem of binge drinking on college campuses. McCardell thinks teens will always find a way to get alcohol; prohibiting them from doing so merely drives their behavior underground, forcing them to drink clandestinely, which usually gets dangerous. "It happens in 'pre-gaming' sessions in locked dorm rooms where students take multiple shots of hard

*When teens drink hand sanitizer and other products to get a buzz, adults are forced to ask themselves: Does withholding alcohol from teens protect them from it or entice them to try anything for a buzz?*

alcohol in rapid succession before going to a social event where alcohol is not served," says McCardell, of students' underground drinking habits. "It happens in off-campus apartments beyond college boundaries and thus beyond the presidents' authority; and it happens in remote fields to which young adults must drive." For McCardell and the 136 college and university presidents who signed the Amethyst Initiative as of June 2012, "alcohol is a reality in the lives of young adults. We can either try to change the reality—which has been our principal focus since 1984, by imposing Prohibition on young adults 18 to 20—or we can create the safest possible environment for the reality."[6]

Underage drinking may be one of those social issues that may never be solved; there is unlikely to be a point at which all underage people abstain from alcohol. Experimenting with alcohol has been a rite of passage for generations, and current and future teens will likely be curious about alcohol and find ways around the law to drink it.

The problem can be managed slowly over time, with the goal of general improvement, though. Managing the issue of underage drinking involves considering the factors that cause teens to drink and also analyzing the harm that comes from it. To this end, the viewpoints presented in *Issues That Concern You: Underage Drinking* consider the benefits and consequences of the twenty-one-and-over drinking age; why teens want to drink; what measures could help them approach alcohol more safely and responsibly; and what role private industry, schools, and parents should play.

## Notes

1. Quoted in Anna Gorman, "A Troubling Trend in Teens Drinking Hand Sanitizer," *Los Angeles Times*, April 24, 2012. http://articles.latimes.com/2012/apr/24/local/la-me-hand-sanitizer-20120424.
2. Stephanie Hayes, "Teens Drinking Hand Sanitizer—Though Underage Drinking Is Down," *Christian Science Monitor*, April 25, 2012. www.csmonitor.com/The-Culture/Family/Modern-Parenthood/2012/0425/Teens-drinking-hand-sanitizer-though-underage-drinking-is-down.
3. Quoted in Meredith Soleau, "You Put What, Up Where? Parents Beware!," Curvy Girl Guide.com, March 9, 2011. www.curvygirlguide.com/parenting/you-put-what-up-where-parents-beware.

4. Joanne Glasser, "Alcohol and Those Under 21 Don't Mix," *Chicago Tribune*, August 29, 2008. http://articles.chicago tribune.com/2008-08-29/news/0808281445_1_underage -drinking-drinking-age-legal-drinking.

5. Sara Huffman, "Would Lowering Legal Drinking Age Curb Campus Binge-Drinking?," *Consumer Affairs*, December 12, 2010. www.consumeraffairs.com/news04/2010/12/would -lowering-legal-drinking-age-curb-campus-binge-drinking .html.

6. John McCardell, "Drinking Age of 21 Doesn't Work," CNN. com, September 16, 2009. http://articles.cnn.com/2009-09-16 /politics/mccardell.lower.drinking.age_1_drinking-age-binge -drinking-federal-highway-appropriation/3?_s=PM:POLITICS.

# ONE

# The State of Underage Drinking in the United States

## Substance Abuse and Mental Health Services Administration

The Substance Abuse and Mental Health Services Administration (SAMHSA), a division of the Department of Health and Human Services of the federal government, prepared the following report for Congress. The report details the state of underage drinking in the United States. On the basis of numerous authoritative studies, the author warns that alcohol abuse is a serious problem among young people. Alcohol is the most widely abused substance among American youth, and binge drinking—the consumption of five or more drinks on one occasion—is particularly common and devastating. They report that girls are beginning to drink as much as boys, that young people are increasingly drinking hard liquor, and that drinking is especially problematic on college campuses. Underage drinking results in fatal car crashes and increased rates of rape, pregnancy, and sexually transmitted disease. For all these reasons SAMHSA advises state governments to make the efforts needed to prevent and reduce underage drinking.

*Report to Congress on the Prevention and Reduction of Underage Drinking: Executive Summary,* Substance Abuse and Mental Health Services Administration (SAMSHA), Department of Health and Human Services, May 2011.

Underage drinking and associated problems have profound negative consequences for underage drinkers, their families, their communities, and society as a whole. Underage drinking contributes to a wide range of costly health and social problems, including motor vehicle crashes (the greatest single mortality risk for underage drinkers); suicide; interpersonal violence (e.g., homicides, assaults, rapes); unintentional injuries such as burns, falls, and drowning; brain impairment; alcohol dependence; risky sexual activity; academic problems; and alcohol and drug poisoning. On average, alcohol is a factor in the deaths of approximately 4,700 youths in the United States per year, shortening their lives by an average of 60 years.

Data show modest reductions in underage drinking and some progress toward the goals of the *Comprehensive Plan to Prevent and Reduce Underage Drinking* but there is still cause for concern. For example, in 2009, 39 percent of 20-year-olds reported binge drinking (drinking at levels substantially increasing the risk of injury or death) in the past 30 days; about 14 percent of 20-year-olds had, in those 30 days, binged five or more times.

Although drinking levels are lower at younger ages, patterns of consumption across the age spectrum pose significant threats to health and well-being. Particularly troubling is the erosion of the traditional gap between underage males and females in binge drinking. This gap is disappearing as females' drinking practices converge with those of males. Thus, females are at increasing risk of alcohol-related mortality and morbidity, including sexual violence.

Still, there is reason for optimism. . . . States are increasingly adopting comprehensive policies and practices to alter the individual and environmental factors that contribute to underage drinking and its consequences; these can be expected to reduce alcohol-related death and disability and associated health care costs. These efforts can potentially reduce underage drinking and its consequences and change norms that support underage drinking in American communities.

## Alcohol Is Most Widely Abused

Alcohol continues to be the most widely used substance of abuse among America's youth, a greater proportion of whom use alcohol than use tobacco or other drugs. For example, according to the 2009 Monitoring the Future study, 30.4 percent of 10th graders reported using alcohol in the past 30 days; 15.9 percent reported marijuana use and 13.1 percent reported cigarette use in the same period.

Binge drinking is the most common underage consumption pattern. High blood alcohol concentrations and impairment levels associated with binge drinking place binge drinkers and those around them at substantially elevated risk for negative consequences. Thus, reducing binge drinking has become a primary public health priority.

Binge rates increase rapidly with age; in 2009 approximately 6.9 million youth 12 to 20 years old (18.1 percent) reported binge drinking in the past month. Although youth generally consume alcohol less frequently and less overall than adults, when they do drink, they are much more likely to binge drink. Accordingly, most youth alcohol consumption occurs in binge drinking episodes. For example, 92 percent of the alcohol consumed by 12- to 14-year-olds is through binge drinking. A significant proportion of underage drinkers consume substantially more than the five-drink binge criterion. For example, averaged 2008 and 2009 data show that 12.1 percent of underage drinkers had nine or more drinks during their last drinking occasion. It is important to note that very young adolescents, because of their smaller size, reach BACs achieved by binge drinking by older adolescents (e.g., age 18 or older) with fewer drinks (3–4 drinks for persons ages 12–15). . . .

## Youth Start Drinking at an Early Age

It is increasingly clear that early initiation to alcohol use is associated with a variety of developmental problems during adolescence as well as problems in later life. These include intentional

*Alcohol is the most widely abused substance among America's youth, a greater proportion of whom use alcohol than tobacco or drugs.*

and unintentional injury to self and others after drinking; violent behavior, including predatory violence and date violence; criminal behavior; prescription drug misuse; unplanned and unprotected sex; motor vehicle crashes and physical fights. Accordingly, increases in the age of alcohol initiation may significantly improve later health.

Although the peak years of initiation to alcohol are 7th to 11th grade, 10 percent of 9- to 10-year-olds have already started drinking and more than one fifth of underage drinkers begin before they are 13 years old. In fact, an estimated 2,842 young people ages 12 to 14 initiated alcohol use per day in 2009. This means slightly more than 1 million (1,038,000) youth under age 15 years initiate alcohol use each year. . . .

Binge drinking rates increase rapidly with age. Approximately 6.9 million youth 12 to 20 years old (18.1 percent) reported binge drinking in the past month. Although youth generally consume alcohol less frequently and less overall than adults, when they do drink, they are much more likely to binge drink: 92 percent of the alcohol consumed by 12- to 14-year-olds is through binge drinking.

**Current and Binge Alcohol Use Among Persons Aged 12 to 20**

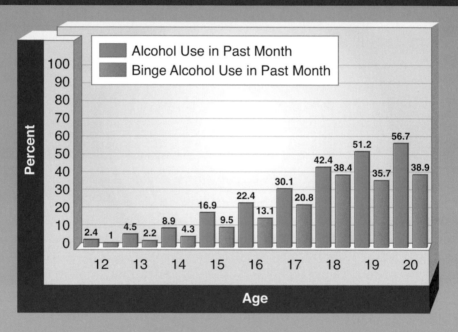

Taken from: *Report to Congress on the Prevention and Reduction of Underage Drinking.* Department of Health and Human Services, Substance Abuse and Mental Health Services Administration (SAMHSA), May 2011. http://store.samhsa.gov/shin/content/SMA11-4645/SMA11-4645.pdf.

## A Pervasive Drinking Culture

Since 1993, youth have reported declines in alcohol availability. However, the number of young people who report that alcohol is fairly easy or very easy to obtain remains high. Very young drinkers are most likely to obtain their alcohol at home from parents, siblings, or storage. It is important to note that some of the methods young people use to obtain alcohol do not violate underage drinking laws in some States.

Eighty-two percent of college students drink and 40 percent report drinking five or more drinks on an occasion in the past 2 weeks. Research indicates that some college students' drinking far exceeds the minimum binge criterion of five drinks per occasion. Although colleges and universities vary widely in student binge drinking rates, overall rates of college student drinking and binge drinking exceed those of non-college-age peers.

Unlike high school students and non-college-age peers, rates of binge drinking among college students have shown little decline since 1993. These differences are not easily attributable to differences between college and non-college-bound students. Although college-bound 12th-graders are consistently less likely than their non-college-bound counterparts to report occasions of heavy drinking, college students report higher rates of binge drinking than college-age youth not attending college. This suggests that the college environment influences drinking practices. . . .

## Underage Drinking Kills

The greatest single mortality risk for underage drinkers is motor vehicle crashes. Mile for mile, teenagers are involved in three times as many fatal crashes as all other drivers. Compared with adults, young people who drink and drive have an increased risk of alcohol-related crashes because of their relative inexperience behind the wheel and their increased impairment from similar amounts of alcohol. One study found that at 0.08 BAC, adult drivers in all age and gender groups compared to sober drivers were 11 times more likely to die in a single vehicle crash. Among those ages 16–20 at 0.08 percent BAC, male drivers were 52 times more likely than sober male drivers the same age to die in a single vehicle fatal crash. In 2008, of the 2,739 young drivers ages 15 to 20 years that were killed in motor vehicle crashes, 694 (25 percent) had a blood alcohol concentration (BAC) of .08 g/dL or higher. According to 2009 survey data, about 3.8 percent of

16-year-olds, 8.7 percent of 17-year-olds, 14.1 percent of 18-year-olds, 17.5 percent of 19-year-olds, and 18.7 percent of 20-year-olds reported driving under the influence of alcohol in the past year.

Homicide and suicide follow motor vehicle crashes as the second and third leading causes of death among teenagers. In 2006, 3,147 young people aged 12–20 died from homicide and 2,220 died from suicide. In addition, 2,332 individuals aged 16–20 died from unintentional injuries other than motor vehicle crashes, such as poisoning, drowning, falls, burns, etc.

At present, it is unclear how many of these deaths are alcohol-related. One study estimated that for all ages combined, nearly a third (31.5 percent) of homicides and almost a quarter (22.7 percent) of suicides were alcohol attributable; they occurred when the decedent had a blood alcohol concentration of 0.10 g/dL or greater. Another study of deaths among those under 21 reported that 12 percent of male suicides and 8 percent of female suicides were alcohol related.

Individuals under the age of 21 commit 45 percent of rapes, 44 percent of robberies, and 37 percent of other assaults; for the population as a whole, an estimated 50 percent of violent crime is related to alcohol use by the perpetrator. The degree to which violent crimes committed by those under 21 are alcohol related is yet unknown.

## Increased Likelihood of Risky Sex

According to the Surgeon General, underage drinking plays a significant role in risky sexual behavior, including unwanted, unintended, and unprotected sexual activity, and sex with multiple partners. Such behavior increases the risk of unplanned pregnancy and sexually transmitted diseases (STDs), including infection with HIV, the virus that causes AIDS. When pregnancies occur, underage drinking may result in fetal alcohol spectrum disorders, including fetal alcohol syndrome, which is a leading cause of mental retardation. Underage drinking by both victim and assailant also increases the risk of physical and sexual assault.

These risks are of particular concern, given the increasing rates of heavy drinking among underage females discussed earlier.

## A Grave Public Health Issue

Underage drinking is a significant public health issue that affects the health and wellbeing of underage drinkers and inflicts heavy financial, physical, and emotional tolls on their families, communities, and society as a whole. Underage alcohol use has proven resistant to change; thus, it is not surprising that progress has been slow.

This report, however, gives reason for optimism, including recent increases in age at first use and reduction of binge drinking. States are increasingly adopting policies and practices to alter individual and environmental factors that contribute to underage drinking and its consequences. These State initiatives, combined with ongoing Federal initiatives, promise meaningful reductions in underage drinking and its consequences and a change in norms that support underage drinking in American communities.

# TWO

# The Drinking Age Should Be Lowered to Eighteen

## Michelle Minton

In the following viewpoint Michelle Minton explains why she thinks the drinking age should be lowered to eighteen. Minton thinks it is unfair that eighteen-year-olds have been deemed mature enough to fight in the military, vote, and get married, but too immature to share a drink with friends. She argues that when teens are exposed to alcohol earlier, they learn to drink slowly, responsibly, and maturely. On the other hand, delaying alcohol consumption leads young people to binge drink and use alcohol without control, with dangerous consequences. Minton says the United States should lower the drinking age to encourage young people both to develop a more responsible and a positive relationship with alcohol at an earlier age and to promote individual liberty.

Minton works at the Competitive Enterprise Institute, an organization that promotes free enterprise and limited government intervention in citizens' lives.

Alaska state representative Bob Lynn (R., Anchorage) is asking the long overdue question: Why do we consider 18-year-olds old enough to join the military, to fight and die for our country, but not to have a drink with their friends before they ship out or while they're home on leave? Lynn has introduced a bill that would allow anyone 18 years and older with a military ID to drink alcohol in Alaska.

The bill is already facing strong opposition from self-styled public-health advocates. However, the data indicate that the 21-minimum drinking age has not only done zero good, it may actually have done harm. In addition, an individual legally enjoys nearly all other rights of adulthood upon turning 18—including the rights to vote, get married, and sign contracts. It is time to reduce the drinking age for all Americans.

## The History of 21-and-Over

In the early 1970s, with the passage of the 26th amendment (which lowered the voting age to 18), 29 states lowered their minimum legal drinking age to 18, 19, or 20 years old. Other states already allowed those as young as 18 to buy alcohol, such as Louisiana, New York, and Colorado. However, after some reports showed an increase in teenage traffic fatalities, some advocacy groups pushed for a higher drinking age. They eventually gained passage of the 1984 National Minimum Drinking Age Act, which lets Congress withhold 10 percent of a state's federal highway funds if it sets its minimum legal drinking age below 21. (Alaska would reportedly lose up to $50 million a year if Lynn's bill passes.)

By 1988, all states had raised their drinking age to 21. In the years since, the idea of lowering the drinking age has periodically returned to the public debate, but groups such as Mothers Against Drunk Driving (MADD) have been able to fight back attempts to change the law. (Louisiana briefly lowered its age limit back to 18 in 1996, after the state Supreme Court ruled that the 21 limit was a form of age discrimination, but the court reversed that decision a few months later.)

## Encouraging Responsible Drinking

It's true that America has a problem with drinking: The rates of alcoholism and teenage problem drinking are far greater here than in Europe. Yet in most European countries, the drinking

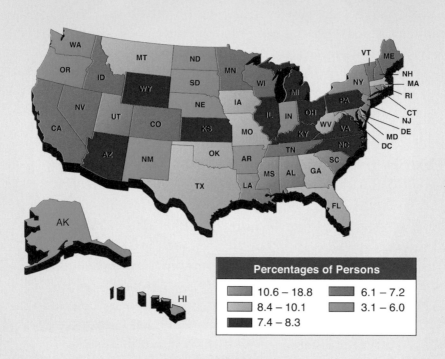

**Percentages of Past Month Drinkers Aged Twelve to Twenty Who Purchased Their Own Alcohol the Last Time They Drank, by State**

Percentages of Persons

- 10.6 – 18.8
- 8.4 – 10.1
- 7.4 – 8.3
- 6.1 – 7.2
- 3.1 – 6.0

Taken from: SAMHSA National Surveys on Drug Use and Health (NSDUHs).

age is far lower than 21. Some, such as Italy, have no drinking age at all. The likely reason for the disparity is the way in which American teens are introduced to alcohol versus their European counterparts. While French or Italian children learn to think of alcohol as part of a meal, American teens learn to drink in the unmonitored environment of a basement or the backwoods with their friends. A 2009 study by the National Institute on Drug Abuse, National Institute of Health, and U.S. Department of Health and Human Services concluded that 72 percent of graduating high-school seniors had already consumed alcohol.

The problem is even worse on college campuses, where there is an unspoken understanding between students, administrators, local law enforcement, and parents that renders drinking-age restrictions effectively moot as students drink alcohol at frat or house parties and in their dorm rooms. The result is dangerous, secret binge drinking. This unspoken agreement and the problems it creates led a group of college chancellors and presidents from around the nation to form the Amethyst Initiative, which proposes a reconsideration of the current drinking age.

Middlebury College president emeritus John M. McCardell, who is also a charter member of Presidents Against Drunk Driving, came out in favor of lowering the drinking age to 18 years old in a 2004 *New York Times* opinion article. "Our latter-day prohibitionists have driven drinking behind closed doors and underground," he wrote. "Colleges should be given the chance to educate students, who in all other respects are adults, in the appropriate use of alcohol, within campus boundaries and out in the open."

## How Many Lives Have Truly Been Saved?

The most powerful argument, at least emotionally, for leaving the drinking age at 21 is that the higher age limit has prevented alcohol-related traffic fatalities. Such fatalities indeed decreased about 33 percent from 1988 to 1998—but the trend is not restricted to the United States. In Germany, for example, where the drinking age is 16, alcohol-related fatalities decreased by 57 percent between 1975 and 1990. The most likely cause for the decrease in traffic fatalities is a combination of law enforcement, education, and advances in automobile-safety technologies such as airbags and roll cages.

In addition, statistics indicate that these fatalities may not even have been prevented but rather *displaced* by three years, and that fatalities might even have increased over the long run because of the reduced drinking age. In an award-winning study in 2010, University of Notre Dame undergraduate Dan Dirscherl found that banning the purchase of alcohol between the ages of 18 and

21 actually *increased* traffic fatalities of those between the ages of 18 and 24 by 3 percent. Dirscherl's findings lend credence to the "experienced drinker" hypothesis, which holds that when people begin driving at 16 and gain confidence for five years before they are legally able to drink, they are more likely to overestimate their driving ability and have less understanding of how alcohol consumption affects their ability to drive.

*Alaska state representative Bob Lynn introduced a bill in the state legislature to allow active-duty armed forces members under the age of twenty-one to buy and drink alcohol.*

## Discriminating Against American Youth

Statistics aside, the drinking age in the U.S. is difficult to enforce and discriminatory toward adults between 18 and 21 years old. The current age limit has created a culture of hidden drinking and disrespect for the law. Regardless of whether an adult is in the military or a civilian, she ought to be treated as just that: an adult. If you are old and responsible enough to go to war, get married, vote, or sign a contract, then you are old and responsible enough to buy a bottle of beer and toast to living in a country that respects and protects individual rights. It is long past time the law caught up with that reality.

# THREE

# The Drinking Age Should Not Be Lowered to Eighteen

**Joanne Glasser**

Joanne Glasser is the president of Bradley University in Peoria, Illinois. In the following viewpoint she argues that the minimum legal drinking age should remain twenty-one, if not higher. Glasser discusses two tragic deaths of Bradley students, neither of which would have been prevented by a lowered drinking age. In her view, alcohol is already too easy for young people to get. She disagrees with other college presidents who have signed the Amethyst Initiative, which lobbies to lower the drinking age. Authorities should make alcohol more difficult to obtain, in her view, not easier, because young people have neither the maturity nor experience to handle alcohol responsibly. She concludes that relaxed alcohol laws will likely contribute to increased injury and death, and thus the drinking age should not be lowered.

About this time last year [summer 2007] a 19-year-old Bradley University soccer player died when four of his friends lit Roman candles, accidentally setting his bedroom on fire as he slept. All had been drinking, including the victim. Three of the four students—who would end up in jail—also played soccer for Bradley.

Eight days after that tragedy I arrived in Peoria [Illinois] to start my first year as Bradley president, knowing well what one of my priorities would be. Bradley would rewrite its book on how to deal with alcohol use and abuse. I did not believe then—nor did the committee members who drafted the new policies conclude—that lives would be saved by dumbing those policies down.

## Making Things Worse

I make this point because more than 120 university presidents have signed on to a movement urging lawmakers to consider lowering the drinking age from 21 to 18. The Amethyst Initiative argues that the higher age limit not only isn't working, it's developed "a culture of dangerous, clandestine binge-drinking" among underage students.

*Raising the drinking age significantly reduced the number of fatal crashes among young people in which alcohol was a factor.*

# Percent of Fifteen- to Sixteen-Year-Olds Reporting Intoxication in the Last Thirty Days*

The United States has a higher drinking age than many European nations, and also is among the nations with lower rates of 15- and 16-year olds who report being drunk within the last month. Some claim this indicates that a higher drinking age helps avoid youth intoxication, which has mulitple consequences.

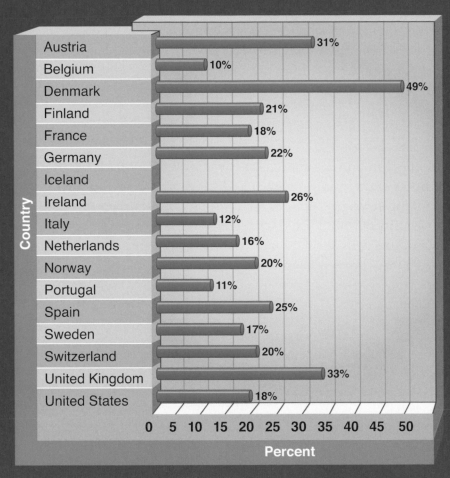

Austria — 31%
Belgium — 10%
Denmark — 49%
Finland — 21%
France — 18%
Germany — 22%
Iceland
Ireland — 26%
Italy — 12%
Netherlands — 16%
Norway — 20%
Portugal — 11%
Spain — 25%
Sweden — 17%
Switzerland — 20%
United Kingdom — 33%
United States — 18%

Country

0  5  10  15  20  25  30  35  40  45  50

**Percent**

*Data on this question not available for Iceland.

Taken from: Bettina Friese and Joel W. Grube. "Youth Drinking Rates and Problems: A Comparison of European Countries and the United States." US Department of Justice, Office of Juvenile Justice and Delinquency Prevention, 2010, pp. 4–5.

I do not believe for a moment that Bradley's tragedy would have been avoided had alcohol been easier to get. And I vehemently disagree that lowering the drinking age would make college campuses safer.

The facts are with me.

The National Highway Traffic Safety Administration says that in 1982, two years before Congress effectively raised the minimum national drinking age, 43 percent of underage drivers involved in fatal crashes had been drinking. By 1998, just 21 percent had been. A NHTSA study found that the new law not only reduced drinking and driving but reduced "youth drinking directly."

## Tougher Enforcement Needed

A 2005 Harvard University study found that binge drinking on college campuses is one-third lower in states where tough laws target high-volume sales. The researchers said states concerned about underage drinking should toughen laws and their enforcement, not ease up.

Reviewing 40 years worth of literature published on the subject, two University of Minnesota researcher concluded, "The preponderance of the evidence suggests that higher legal drinking ages reduce alcohol consumption."

One of the leading experts on the misuse of alcohol by college students, Henry Wechsler of the Harvard School of Public Health, says reducing the drinking age would not reduce the misuse of alcohol on college campuses.

The American Medical Association [AMA] seconds that conclusion: "There is no evidence that there were fewer campus alcohol problems when lower drinking ages were in effect." Conversely, universities have found that the minimum legal drinking age "provides a strong legal rationale to develop effective prevention policies that can reduce high-risk as well as underage drinking," according to the AMA.

## Protecting Students from Alcohol Abuse

That is exactly what we have done at Bradley University.

Some highlights:

- Weekend, on-campus events dubbed "Late Night BU" provide our students with alcohol-free ways to have fun.
- Our alcohol education program has been expanded and integrated into first-year classes and residence hall programs.

New penalties underscore just how seriously we take alcohol misuse. Students who violate our policy may be fined and may be prohibited from living in fraternity or sorority houses, or elsewhere off campus. Student leaders who are twice cited will be barred from holding leadership positions for a year. Repeat offenders may be suspended from the university.

Ask me to describe Bradley, and I'll tell you it's a superb university for serious students, located in a prototypical American city. In coping with an "alcohol culture" on campus, Bradley is the norm, not the exception. What's unusual at Bradley is our determination to change that—and our motivation. I should say that Bradley University doesn't make anyone's list of the nation's top party schools.

## Alcohol Kills

Not long after our committee began meeting, alcohol played a major role in the death of another student: a young man who fell into traffic while horsing around along a busy street near campus. His blood-alcohol content was more than twice Illinois' legal threshold. This student was 22, one year past the minimum drinking age. Clearly the fact that he could access alcohol legally did not protect him from misusing it.

Because of what Bradley went through this past year, I believe I may recognize more than most the serious consequences of allowing 18- and 19-year-olds to belly up to the bar, no questions asked. Our plan is intended both to make a meaningful difference at Bradley and to make the university a national leader in combating the misuse of alcohol. We will be measuring changes in students' perceptions and behavior to see how we're doing. We'll be happy to keep you posted.

# FOUR

# Eliminating the Drinking Age Promotes Freedom

Jeffrey A. Tucker

The drinking age should be eliminated entirely argues Jeffrey A. Tucker in the following viewpoint. Tucker discusses alcohol's long and varied history in the United States. He points out that at the country's founding, there were no federal laws regarding alcohol; families, churches, and communities morally regulated drinking. When the government got involved in alcohol legislation, Tucker argues, it was an abject failure: Crime and consumption skyrocketed. Tucker suggests that overly strict drinking laws beg to be broken and are the cause of many of society's problems with alcohol. Eliminating the drinking age would help people develop a personalized, responsible relationship with alcohol while respecting individual liberty and freedom, he concludes.

Tucker is the author of *Bourbon for Breakfast: Living Outside the Statist Quo* and *It's a Jetsons World: Private Miracles and Public Crimes*. He is a consultant to the Ludwig von Mises Institute and a commentator on the institute's website.

Somehow, and no one seems to even imagine how, this country managed to survive and thrive before 1984 without a national minimum drinking age. Before that, the drinking question was left to the states.

## Twenty-One-and-Over Violates Freedom

In the 19th century, and looking back even before—prepare yourself to imagine horrific anarchistic nightmares—there were no drinking laws anywhere, so far as anyone can tell. The regulation of drinking and age was left to society, which is to say families, churches, and communities with varying sensibilities who regulated such things with varying degrees of intensity. Probably some kids drank themselves silly—and we all know that this doesn't happen now (wink, wink)—but many others learned to drink responsibly from an early age, even drinking bourbon for breakfast.

Really, it is only because we are somehow used to it that we accept the complete absurdity of a national law that prohibits the sale of beer, wine, and liquor to anyone under the age of 21. This is a restriction unknown in the developed world. Most countries set 18 as the limit, and countries like Germany and Austria allow 16-year-olds to buy wine and beer. In the home of the brave, the police are busting up teen parties, shutting down bars, hectoring restaurants, fining convenience stores, and otherwise bullying people into clean living. We read the news and think: crazy kids, they shouldn't be doing this.

## Drinking Age Laws Beg to Be Broken

And yet every day, young people are finding ways around these preposterous restrictions that are hardly ever questioned, imbibing with their booze a disdain for the law and a creative spirit of criminality, along with a disposition to binge drink when their legal workarounds succeed.

On college campuses, the industry of the fake ID thrives as never before. It seems nearly true that almost every student believes himself or herself in need of getting one. Do the restaurants and bars know this? Of course they do. They have every interest in having these fake IDs look as real as possible to give themselves some degree of legal immunity if someone gets caught. The whole thing is a gigantic fakeroo, a mass exercise in open but unspoken hypocrisy, and everyone knows it.

If you think about it, it is the very definition of a state gone mad that a society would have a law of this sort spread out over an entire nation that tells people that they cannot drink before the age of 21—even as most everyone in a position to do so happily breaks the law. In Virginia, in the colonial period, where the average lifespan was 25, this law would have provided only 4 years of drinking in the last fifth of one's life (but what a way to go).

## Prohibitions on Alcohol Always Fail

However, if you think about the history of this country in the twentieth century, one might say that the age of 21 is actually rather liberal, as strange as that may sound. After all, it was in this country, the "land of the free," that the federal government actually added as part of its Constitution a total banning of liquor, wine, and beer from sea to shining sea (1920 to 1933). The 1920s roared, in any case, with organized crime, speakeasies, police corruption, rampant criminality, and alcohol abuse.

The mystery to me is not the failure of Prohibition but the sheer insanity of the attempt to do this in the first place. It seems utterly bizarre in a country that habitually proclaims its devotion to liberty and freedom that such a thing would have ever been attempted. But here is Amendment XVIII, passed in 1917, in the same epoch in which government was going to rid the world of despotism and stabilize all business cycle through scientific monetary policy:

> The manufacture, sale, or transportation of intoxicating liquors within, the importation thereof into, or the exportation thereof from the United States and all territory subject to the jurisdiction thereof for beverage purposes is hereby prohibited.

## Europe Lets Young People Buy Alcohol Sooner than the United States

The United States has a higher legal purchasing age than nearly every country in Europe.

| Country | Age | Country | Age |
|---------|-----|---------|-----|
| Armenia | 16 | Lithuania | 18 |
| Austria | 16 | Malta | 16 |
| Belgium | 15 | Netherlands | 16 |
| Bulgaria | 16 | Norway | 18 |
| Croatia | 18 | Poland | 18 |
| Czech | 18 | Portugal | 18 |
| Denmark | 18 | Russia | 21 |
| Estonia | 18 | Slovak Republic | 18 |
| Finland | 16 | Slovenia | 18 |
| Germany | 16 | Spain | 16 |
| Greece | 18 | Sweden | 18 |
| Hungary | 18 | Switzerland | 14 |
| Iceland | 20 | Ukraine | 21 |
| Ireland | 18 | United Kingdom | 18 |
| Italy | 16 | United States | 21 |
| Latvia | 18 | | |

Taken from: Bettina Friese and Joel W. Grube. "Youth Drinking Rates and Problems: A Comparison of European Countries and the United States." US Department of Justice, Office of Juvenile Justice and Delinquency Prevention, 2010, p. 3.

Yes, it really happened, right here in the good ol' USA, and I'm grateful to Mark Thornton for documenting the politics and economics of the whole sad affair in his book *The Economics of Prohibition*. In a rare case of reversion and admission of error, the same constitution was later amended again: "The eighteenth article of amendment to the Constitution of the United States is hereby repealed."

## Growing Conservatism Hurts Freedom

But the habit of prohibition was already ingrained. For the state, it was two steps forward and one step back. For the rest of the population, what was previously a very normal part of life—drinking potentially intoxicating liquids, something integral to normal living from the Paleolithic era forward—took on a special ethos of hipness and derring-do. The father of our country might have been the largest distiller of whiskey in the late 1700s, but after Prohibition, liquor took on associations of decadence and bad behavior generally. A distiller today wouldn't be elected to the city council much less as the US President.

Now, it wasn't too many years ago that the laws tended to be a bit more reasonable, with the drinking age starting at 18. But that was changed with a universal law for the age of 21, and many people remember what this was like: for two years, a person was able to order a beer with a burger and, then one day, doing the same thing was a criminal act.

## Teens, Alcohol, and Driving

Digging around for explanations about these silly laws, there is one overarching argument: driving. We don't want drunken teenagers on the road. These laws have saved thousands, millions, of lives, and the desire to change them is the equivalent of harboring a death wish for a generation. Now, one libertarian response might be: then get rid of the public roads and let road owners manage whether and to what extent its drivers drink. That's a principled position but a bit impractical. The biggest problem with that response is that it concedes too much.

The closer you look at these studies, the fishier they appear. It turns out that most of the declines in binge drinking among high-school kids, according to a trends in drug use report, took place before the change in the law, and, according [to] researchers Jeffrey A. Miron and Elina Tetelbaum, the changes in trends after are heavily biased by data sampling from a single state. Therefore, data on drunk driving, whatever the trends, cannot be statistically attributed to the national minimum-drinking-age law.

In any case, "underage" drinking is still sky high, even with the law, making cause and effect even more difficult to trace. As to why drinking is still high among college students, the National Institute on Drug Abuse offers the following polite reason: "Campuses provided some insulation from the effects of changes in the drinking age laws that took place during that interval." You can say that again. Human beings are remarkable things: when they want to do something, no amount of tyranny, even that of jail, can stop them.

## Alcohol Not to Blame for All Problems

Still, it is impossible to silence the screams of the prohibition advocates, who trace every car accident among teen drivers to alcohol. I find this all fascinating to read because it bears so much in common with the Prohibition literature from the 1910s and 1920s. Their propaganda blamed alcohol for the destruction of the family, the persistence of poverty, the high rate of crime, the problem of illiteracy, and the ubiquity of sin generally. Clearly, their arguments were widely accepted even though it is all a big and fallacious mix-up of cause and effect. It's not that liquor caused all these terrible things; it's that the people who engage in terrible behaviors tend to also be drinkers. Abolishing the drink won't fix the problems of the human heart.

So it is with teenage drinking. With the two thirds and more of people under the age of 21 reporting that they have consumed alcohol in the last year, it should be obvious that the law is doing nothing but providing a gigantic excuse for arbitrary police-state impositions on human liberty, and also socializing young people in a habit of hypocrisy and law breaking. It's like the old Soviet-style joke: they pretend to regulate us and we pretend to be regulated.

Still, shouldn't it be illegal for young people to drink and drive? Murray Rothbard sums up the libertarian point in *For A New Liberty*:

Only the overt commission of a crime should be illegal, and the way to combat crimes committed under the influence of alcohol is to be more diligent about the crimes themselves, not to outlaw the alcohol. And this would have the further beneficial effect of reducing crimes *not* committed under the influence of alcohol.

## Eliminate the Drinking Age Entirely

We've just been through our annual celebration of Independence Day, the day on which every radio and television commentator gives pious speeches about the glories of American liberty and all the sacrifices that have been made to preserve it.

*A large collection of confiscated fake IDs testifies to the ease with which they can be obtained by underaged youth.*

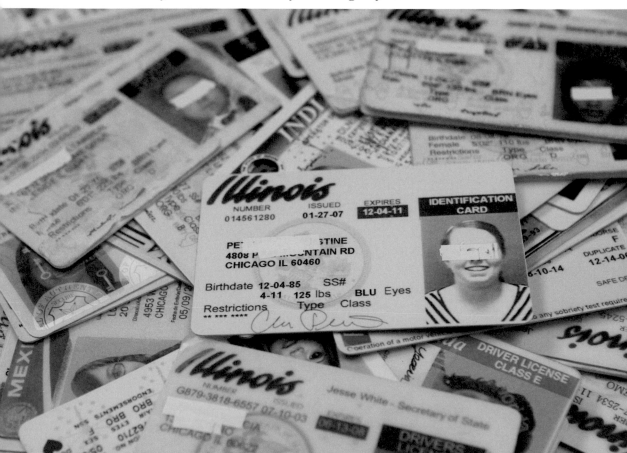

Do we really believe it? The founders would have never imagined such a thing as a national law regulating the age at which beer, wine, port, and other alcoholic beverages are consumed. If we are serious about embracing their vision of a free society, as opposed to just blathering about it, let's start with something that is supremely practical and would have immediate effects on an entire generation: repeal the national minimum-drinking-age law.

You say that this is unthinkable? I say that you don't really believe in human liberty.

# FIVE

# Eliminating or Lowering the Drinking Age Will Cost Lives

## Robert A. Corrigan

> Robert A. Corrigan is the president of San Francisco State University. In the following viewpoint he argues the drinking age should not be eliminated because doing so will cost many young lives. Corrigan explains that before the drinking age was set at twenty-one, alcohol-related traffic fatalities were higher than when the drinking age was raised. Going back to a lower drinking age would likely mean a return to an increase in drunk driving deaths, he argues. As a college president, Corrigan believes that discouraging alcohol use helps young people make positive choices of which they can be proud. Conversely, alcohol abuse results in poor choices, including drunk driving, sexual assault, or humiliating and degrading behavior. For all of these reasons, Corrigan concludes the twenty-one-and-over drinking age protects young people and helps them get through their college years safely and smartly.

Universities exist to improve lives. Faculty, administrators and staff devote their careers to helping people—many of them young people—to fulfill their promise.

Nothing is more difficult for us to bear than the loss of a student, cut down in his or her prime because of an accident, illness or poor choice. And we know, from years of experience, that one major path toward making poor choices is excessive consumption of alcohol.

Yes, college is an important time to learn lessons not only about history, science, literature and art, but about life. There simply are some lessons that 18-to-20-year-olds—away from home and parental supervision for the first time in their lives—simply should not have to master: accompanying a classmate to the ER [emergency room] for treatment of an alcohol overdose; waking to a partner in bed and no recollection of what transpired there; grieving for a friend killed in an auto accident where alcohol was involved.

*A student in an alcohol-education program wears vision-distorting goggles while making her way through an obstacle course in a wheelchair. The exercise gives students a simulated experience of driving while impaired by alcohol.*

## A Lower Drinking Age Will Increase Deaths

If our nation reduces the drinking age from 21 to 18, as a coalition of university leaders has proposed, we will turn our campuses into the wrong kind of learning labs. The National Highway Traffic Safety Administration says that since 1975, laws setting the drinking age at 21 have cut traffic fatalities among 18-to-20-year-old drivers by 13 percent, saving an estimated 19,121 lives. That is a huge number of promising lives that could be cut short by lowering the drinking age—a little more than twice the number of new freshmen at S.F. State and Cal Berkeley this year [2008].

The Centers for Disease Control and Prevention estimates lowering the drinking age to 18 will increase fatalities by 10 percent. The American Medical Association reports that the brains of adolescents are so vulnerable that even short-term or moderate drinking can impair memory, learning, information recall and socialization—some of the very reasons for which we send our youth to college.

We take a strong stand against underage drinking at S.F. State, as do all 23 campuses in the California State University system. Our trustees adopted a comprehensive alcohol policy in 2001 that applies to students of all ages. It is considered the most comprehensive alcohol policy of any university system in the country—and it works.

## Alcohol-Related Motor Vehicle Crashes

The greatest single mortality risk for underage drinkers is motor vehicle crashes. Mile for mile, teenagers are involved in three times as many fatal crashes as all other drivers. Compared with adults, young people who drink and drive have an increased risk of alcohol-related crashes because of their relative inexperience behind the wheel and their increased impairment from similar amounts of alcohol.

### Leading Causes of Death for Teens

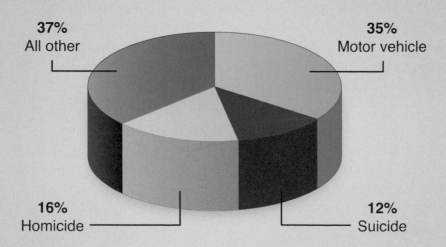

**37%**
All other

**35%**
Motor vehicle

**16%**
Homicide

**12%**
Suicide

Taken from: *Report to Congress on the Prevention and Reduction of Underage Drinking.* Department of Health and Human Service, Substance Abuse and Mental Health Services Administration (SAMHSA), May 2011. http://store.samhsa.gov/shin/content/SMA11-4645/SMA11-4645.pdf.

## Tighter Legislation Protects Young People

Since the policy was adopted, campuses report a decrease in students driving after consuming alcohol and DUIs [citations for driving under the influence of alcohol]; fewer incidents of alcohol-related misconduct; reduced underage drinking and reduced binge drinking.

Here at S.F. State, all incoming first-year students participate in mandatory alcohol-education training that prepares them to make well-informed decisions about alcohol. Our campus health service has an active, multifaceted alcohol-education program that teaches students about alcohol and other drugs, provides support services for all students grappling with substance related problems and offers assessment, counseling and referrals. Our University Police Department actively patrols not just the campus, but surrounding neighborhoods to enforce legal behavior and neighborly parties.

## Let Young People Fulfill Their Promise

Despite our efforts, and a drinking age of 21, we still have occasions where students drink excessively and make dangerous choices. Consider that half of the sexual assaults reported on our campus last year involved excessive alcohol consumption by victims under 21. Consider that we still witness alcohol overdoses, still break up parties where legal IDs are in short supply, still catch an occasional driver who can't pass one of college's most important tests—a sobriety test. A change in federal law that enlarges the pool of college students who can legally drink simply won't help.

Let's keep our young people focused on fulfilling their great personal promise. Keep the drinking age at 21, and give our youth the time and support needed to learn about life, social norms and keeping alcohol in perspective.

# SIX

# Lowering the Drinking Age Can Prevent Binge Drinking

Morris E. Chafetz

Binge drinking can be reduced or prevented by lowering the drinking age, argues Morris E. Chafetz in the following viewpoint. Chafetz discusses his involvement in setting the minimum drinking age at twenty-one in the 1980s, saying it is the single most regrettable act of his entire career. In his view, alcohol is not the problem; immature, irresponsible drinkers are. The way to help drinkers become more responsible, according to Chafetz, is to familiarize them with alcohol at an earlier age. Young people are not going to stop wanting to try alcohol, so Chafetz thinks withholding alcohol from them forces them to drink without guidance or maturity. He concludes that lowering the drinking age would offer young people an appropriate environment in which to experiment safely with alcohol.

Chafetz founded the National Institute on Alcohol Abuse and Alcoholism in 1970. He was a former member of the Presidential Commission on Drunk Driving and a director and executive member of the National Commission Against Drunk Driving until his death in 2011.

In 1982 I accepted appointment to the Presidential Commission on Drunk Driving and agreed to chair its Education and Prevention Committee. The Commission met over the next 18 months and ultimately advanced 39 recommendations to President [Ronald] Reagan, in December 1983. All 39 received unanimous Commission approval.

The most conspicuous of those recommendations, and arguably the most controversial, called for raising the minimum legal drinking age to 21 nationwide. I will admit to having had serious reservations about this particular proposal. But in the interest of maintaining unanimity, I reluctantly voted yes.

It is the single most regrettable decision of my entire professional career.

## Correlation Is Not Cause

Legal Age 21 has not worked. To be sure, drunk driving fatalities are lower now than they were in 1982. But they are lower in all age groups. And they have declined just as much in Canada, where the age is 18 or 19, as they have in the United States.

It has been argued that "science" convincingly shows a cause-and-effect relationship between the law and the reduction in fatalities. Complicated mathematical formulas, which include subjective estimations (called "imputation") have been devised to demonstrate "proof." But correlation is not cause. We must neither confuse numbers with science nor interpret a lack of numbers as implying an absence of science.

But even if we concede that the law has had some effect on our highways, we cannot overlook its collateral, off-road damage. The National Institute for Alcoholism and Alcohol Abuse, which I founded in 1970, estimates that 5,000 lives are lost to alcohol each year by those under 21. More than 3,000 of those fatalities occur off our roadways. If we are seriously to measure the effects of this law, we cannot limit our focus.

## Kids Drink to Get Drunk

And if we broaden our look, we see a serious problem of reckless, goal-oriented, drinking to get drunk. Those at whom the law is directed disobey it routinely. Enforcement is frustratingly difficult and usually forces the behavior deeper underground, into places where life and health are put at ever greater risk. The 600,000 assaults reported annually, the date rapes, the property damage, the emergency room calls do not in general occur in places visible to the public. They are the inevitable result of what happens when laws do not reflect social or cultural reality.

The reality is that at age 18 in this country, one is a legal adult. Young people view 21 as utterly arbitrary—which it is. And because the explanation given them is so condescending—that they lack maturity and judgment, these same people who can serve on juries and sign contracts and who turned out in overwhelming numbers to elect our first black president—well, they don't buy it.

And neither do I. And neither should the American public.

*A neighborhood memorial for a dead teen is seen here. The National Institute on Alcohol Abuse and Alcoholism estimates that five thousand underage lives are lost to alcohol each year.*

## Drinking Earlier Is Probably Safer

Whether we like it or not, alcohol is woven into the fabric of our world, most of which has determined that the legal drinking age should be 18—or lower. And so far as I can tell, there is no evidence of massive brain impairment, alcohol dependency, or underage alcohol abuse, which the "experts" tell us will be the inevitable result of lowering the age in the United States.

It is time to liberate ourselves from the tyranny of "experts," who invoke "science" in order to advance a prohibitionist agenda. Prohibition does not work. It has never worked. It is not working among 18–20 year-olds now.

The cult of expertise has made parents feel incapable of raising their children. In many states parents are disenfranchised from helping their sons or daughters learn about responsible alcohol consumption. But as a parent and psychiatrist I trust the instinct of parents more than I do the hubris of "experts."

## The Problem Is the Drinker, Not the Drink

Despite what these latter-day prohibitionists may think, the problem is not the drink—it is the drinker. There should be more emphasis on the person and the surroundings in which alcohol is consumed and less emphasis on alcohol itself. Personal and social responsibility, not the substance, is the real issue.

But so long as the age remains a one-size-fits-all, federally-mandated 21, and so long as any state that may want to try something different, in hopes of reversing the dismal trend of binge-drinking that (maybe or maybe not coincidentally) has become more serious in the years since the drinking age was raised, forfeits 10% of its federal highway funds, nothing is likely to change for the better.

I do not believe that any state should be forced to adjust its drinking age. But I do believe that the genius of federalism should be allowed to work its will unimpeded, and from that genius, not only better practices, but also safer environments and more responsible consumption, are likely to emerge.

# SEVEN

# Lowering the Drinking Age Will Encourage Binge Drinking

Sara Huffman

Sara Huffman is a contributor to *Consumer Affairs*, which originally published this viewpoint. In it, Huffman argues that lowering the drinking age would worsen the problem of binge drinking on college campuses and elsewhere. She discusses the findings of a study that simulated the effects of a lowered drinking age on binge drinking. Researchers found that on campuses where underage drinking laws were enforced and the majority of students had normal perceptions of the drinking behaviors of their peers, a lowered drinking age would result in more binge drinking. Huffman concludes that making alcohol more available to young people is more likely to worsen, not improve, binge drinking and other problematic behaviors.

Perhaps they get an "A" for effort, but a push from university presidents to lower the legal drinking age to 18 fails several crucial tests.

In 2008, a group of college presidents and chancellors formed the Amethyst Initiative, a call to rethink the current minimum legal drinking age of 21, citing it would cut down on binge-drinking. They argue that the law encourages underage college students to drink at parties, where binge drinking is common. The main argument states [that] if students as young as 18 could legally drink in bars and restaurants, they might instead learn more-moderate drinking habits, which could then lead to less binge drinking on college campuses. So far, 135 college presidents have signed the Initiative's public statement urging lawmakers to reconsider the legal drinking age.

## A Risky Experiment

But to simply lower the drinking age without an understanding of its effects would constitute a "radical experiment," said Richard A. Scribner, M.D., M.P.H., of the Louisiana State University

*Researchers have found that the college campuses most likely to see a decline in binge drinking due to a lower drinking age were those that had the poorest enforcement of underage drinking laws.*

# The Legal Drinking Age Works

Congress passed the National Minimum Drinking Age Act in 1984, which established twenty-one as the minimum legal drinking age. Supporters say the law works because since then, teen drinking is down and teen binge drinking is down.

## High School Seniors' Alcohol Use Declines

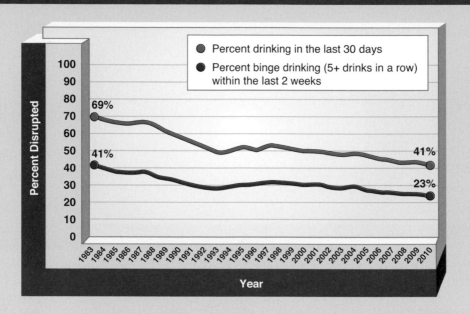

Taken from: *The Monitoring the Future National Survey Results on Drug Use, 1975–2010.* Available at monitoringthefuture.org; and dontserveteens.gov.

School of Public Health (http://publichealth.lsubsc.edu/), one of the researchers on a new study in the January issue of the *Journal of Studies on Alcohol and Drugs*.

Scribner and his colleagues at BioMedware Corporation in Ann Arbor, MI, along with other institutions found a way to test this "radical experiment" without involving any actual drinking. They used a mathematical model to estimate the effects that a lower drinking age would have on college binge drinking.

The model, based on survey data from students at 32 U.S. colleges, aimed to evaluate the "misperception effect" emphasized by the Amethyst Initiative—that is, the idea that underage students widely perceive "normal" drinking levels to be higher than they actually are and that students would adjust their own habits if they were surrounded by social drinkers rather than binge-drinking party-goers.

Overall, the researchers found the campuses that were most likely to see a decline in binge drinking from a lowered legal drinking age were those that had the poorest enforcement of underage drinking laws—being surrounded, for instance, by bars that do not check identification—and a significant level of student misperception of "normal" drinking (that is, students thinking that the average fellow student drinks much more than he or she actually does).

## Increased Binge Drinking

If misperception levels were not present or were at the levels shown by the survey data, these campuses would likely see more binge-drinking if the legal age were lowered. On "drier" campuses, the study found, student misperceptions would have to be even greater.

"The higher the level of enforcement of underage drinking laws, the higher the level of misperception would have to be for the Amethyst Initiative to have any hope of being effective," explained lead researcher Dr. Jawaid W. Rasul, of BioMedware Corporation. "The misperception effect would have to be extremely large." And without data supporting the existence of such high levels of student misperception, Rasul said, lowering the legal drinking age would be unlikely to curb college binge drinking.

Scribner also pointed out that lowering the drinking age would not only affect college students but all currently underage young adults.

And past research has suggested that when alcohol becomes more readily accessible to young people, alcohol-related problems, such as drunk driving, go up.

# EIGHT

# Exposing Teens to Alcohol Helps Them Drink Responsibly

**Elizabeth Hanna**

In the following viewpoint Elizabeth Hanna argues that the twenty-one-and-over drinking age discourages young people from developing a responsible relationship with alcohol. She explains how her parents allowed her to taste alcohol early in life, which helped her approach drinking in a sensible manner. According to Hanna, prohibitions on alcohol glorify drinking because they make young people overly curious and excited about it. When young people are finally of age to drink, they do so without caution, respect, or guidance. Hanna says alcohol-related problems have more to do with society's loose values and human beings' tendency to sin, not with alcohol itself. She concludes that reducing or eliminating the drinking age will help young people drink responsibly and avoid the many problems that come with unfettered alcohol use.

Hanna graduated from the University of Georgia in 2012 and is a writer for the website New Feminism.

I had my first taste of alcohol on vacation with my parents when I was eight years old. We had just sat down to dinner at a restaurant in Rome, and the waiter came as usual to pour wine for my parents. To my surprise, he didn't pass over my glass. As I looked at him, puzzled, he threw his hands up and exclaimed some Italian version of, "Well, why not?" My parents explained to me that, in Italy, children were allowed to drink wine. I shrugged, unaware of the political and moral controversies, and took a sip.

My most recent experience with alcohol was accompanying my boyfriend to the package store as he legally bought his first bottle of wine. Though he was well past the drafting age, he was nevertheless "underage" when it came to drinking. As we roamed through the aisles, we couldn't help laughing at both the excitement and absurdity of this 21-year-old rite of passage.

## Drinking Age Laws Glorify Alcohol

Unfortunately, the legal drinking age has only glorified the appeal of alcohol consumption and muddled our conception of what ought to be our boundaries, and who or what should be blamed when we cross them.

The truth is, alcohol is a blessing, and we should be careful where we place our blame when we abuse it. By faulting alcohol itself, we curse a beautiful gift, thus offending the Giver and denying the true source of the problem. Alcohol abuse isn't an inherent consequence of alcohol, but rather a manifestation of our own tendency to sin. (Alcoholism is a physical and psychological ailment, and I don't mean to take it lightly; the abuse I'm describing is carried out by those *without* such circumstances.) When we willingly drink to excess, we reject the natural law and the proper ordering of things, making a false god out of a created good. Along with its own inherent vice, drunkenness becomes a social crutch, an opening to addiction to both the circumstances surrounding it and to the alcohol itself, and an avenue for further foolishness. If we want to deal with the issue of alcohol abuse, we need to first address our own sinful natures before resorting to laws that create more problems than they solve.

## The Unfairness of 21-and-Over

There is a contradiction at the heart of the drinking age restriction. An 18-year-old can join the military to fight and possibly

# Where Do Underage Drinkers Get Alcohol?

Data from the National Survey on Drug Use and Health show that 93.4 percent of adolescents who drank in the last month received their alcohol for free the last time they drank, and 44.8 percent (about 317,000) got alcohol for free from their family or at home. These results suggest that family members can play a direct role in influencing young people's relationship with alcohol.

## Payment and Source of Most Recently Used Alcohol Among Past Month Users Aged Twelve to Fourteen

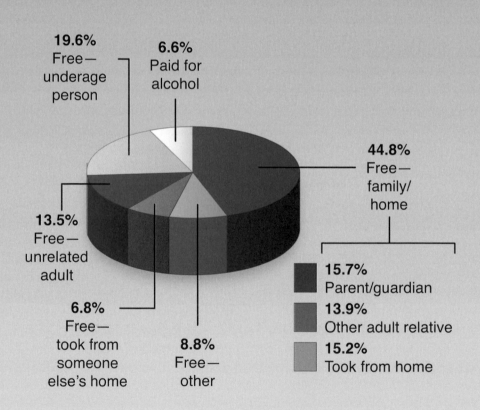

19.6%
Free—
underage
person

6.6%
Paid for
alcohol

44.8%
Free—
family/
home

13.5%
Free—
unrelated
adult

6.8%
Free—
took from
someone
else's home

8.8%
Free—
other

15.7%
Parent/guardian

13.9%
Other adult relative

15.2%
Took from home

Taken from: The National Survey on Drug Use and Health (NSDUH). Substance Abuse and Mental Health Services Administration, 2011.

die for his country, but he can't drink a beer to celebrate his send-off. One can get drug prescriptions—even an abortion—before the 21st birthday. Even a junior high school student can readily buy glue, scissors, insecticide, and cleaning detergent—all more potentially dangerous than alcohol. Nor is there any necessary reason to assume that a 13-year-old would exercise less temperance with alcohol than a 21-year-old. It depends entirely on *which* 13-year-old and *which* 21-year-old we're talking about.

By tossing open the gates to inebriation at a time when young adults are away from parental guidance, the drinking age restriction actually undercuts the important socialization that leads to the mature use of alcohol. I have countless peers whose parents did not allow them to drink "until college," or their 21st birthdays. Now, cut loose in an environment not known for moderation, many of those kids are spending their Friday nights passed out. This was entirely predictable. The law, in its current state of loose implementation, allows for kids who would have been going wild already to take it to the next level with the invigorating sense of rebellion or "finally getting to have fun."

## Values, Not Laws, Encourage Moderation

Alcohol is neither a demon nor a god. I grew up drinking when my parents would drink (this is legal, by the way). Intoxication was not the goal—the idea never even entered my mind, since I never saw *them* using alcohol that way. I had been taught by example that alcohol was a nice additive to life, nothing more and nothing less.

Some argue that lowering or eliminating the drinking age would result in a surge of alcoholism, and suddenly the bars would be flush with hammered 18-year-olds. I hate to break it to the critics, but that's already the case (hence the term "freshmen bar"). Most likely, the anticipated craziness following a drinking law repeal would die down after a few nights—a semester at most for the easier college majors. As for those young people who might drink too much, they are doing so already. Criminalizing a broad behavior just to eliminate its *abuse* misses the target.

*Some find it unfair that an eighteen-year-old soldier can die for his or her country but cannot legally drink a beer before being sent off to war.*

Would prohibiting sex get rid of sex offenders? Of course not. It would simply mean that only sex offenders would be having sex.

Prohibition turned drunkards into moonshiners, and we still haven't learned. By scapegoating a healthy substance because of some individuals' misuse of it, we both encourage the abuse and miss the real problem. Once we acknowledge the role of sin in all of this, we can begin to teach (by example, where possible) the virtue of moderation and learn to obey the Laws that matter most.

# NINE

# Teen Drinking May Cause Irreversible Brain Damage

Michelle Trudeau

Teen drinking may cause irreversible brain damage, Michelle Trudeau reports in the following viewpoint. She discusses a study by researchers at University of California–San Diego, which found damaged brain tissue in teens who drank alcohol. Alcohol consumption on developing brain tissue appeared to impede boys' attention span, ruining their ability to focus over time. Girl subjects, meanwhile, demonstrated a worsened ability to comprehend visual information. In both boys and girls, researchers found evidence of damaged brain tissue, which may be irreversible. The study's results may be used to argue that young people should be discouraged from drinking and that the drinking age should remain at twenty-one years old.

Trudeau is a reporter for National Public Radio, where this story was originally broadcast.

For teenagers, the effects of a drunken night out may linger long after the hangover wears off. A study led by neuroscientist Susan Tapert of the University of California, San Diego compared the brain scans of teens who drink heavily with the scans of teens who don't.

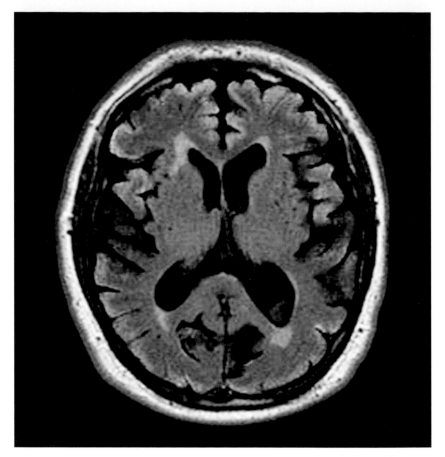

*The long-term effects of alcohol abuse on the brain are shown in this magnetic resonance imaging (MRI) scan. The black areas show where the brain has shrunk, causing loss of memory, confusion, impaired judgment, and personality changes.*

Tapert's team found damaged nerve tissue in the brains of the teens who drank. The researchers believe this damage negatively affects attention span in boys, and girls' ability to comprehend and interpret visual information. "First of all, the adolescent brain is still undergoing several maturational processes that render it more vulnerable to some of the effects of substances," Tapert says. In other words, key areas of the brain are still under construction during the adolescent years, and are more sensitive to the toxic effects of drugs and alcohol.

For the study, published last month in the journal *Psychology of Addictive Behaviors*, Tapert looked at 12- to 14-year-olds before they used any alcohol or drugs. Over time, some of the kids started to drink, a few rather heavily—consuming four or five drinks per occasion, two or three times a month—classic binge drinking behavior in teens.

Comparing the young people who drank heavily with those who remained non-drinkers, Tapert's team found that the binge drinkers did worse on thinking and memory tests. There was also a distinct gender difference. "For girls who had been engaging in heavy drinking during adolescence, it looks like they're performing more poorly on tests of spatial functioning, which links to mathematics, engineering kinds of functions," Tapert says.

And the boys?

"For boys who engaged in binge drinking during adolescence, we see poor performance on tests of attention—so being able to focus on something that might be somewhat boring, for a sustained period of time," Tapert says. "The magnitude of the difference is 10 percent. I like to think of it as the difference between an A and a B."

## Teenage Tendency to Experiment to Blame

Pediatrician and brain researcher Ron Dahl from the University of Pittsburgh notes that adolescents seem to have a higher tolerance for the negative immediate effects of binge drinking, such as feeling ill and nauseated. "Which makes it easier to consume higher amounts and enjoy some of the positive aspects," Dahl says. "But, of course, that also creates a liability for the spiral of addiction and binge use of these substances."

He adds that there is a unique feature of the teenage brain that drives much behavior during adolescence: The teen brain is primed and ready for intense, all-consuming learning. "Becoming passionate about a particular activity, a particular sport, passionate about literature or changing the world or a particular religion" is a normal, predictable part of being a teenager, he says. "But those same tendencies to explore and try new things and try on

# How Alcohol Affects the Teenage Brain

Drinking alcohol during times of peak plasticity can damage brain wiring.

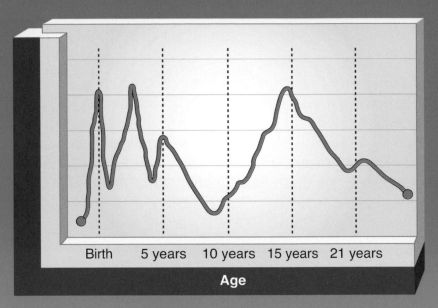

**Peaks of Brain Plasticity**

Age: Birth, 5 years, 10 years, 15 years, 21 years

Taken from: "Underage Drinking." Speak Up! Prevention Coalition, 2011.

new identities may also increase the likelihood of starting on negative pathways," he adds.

## Damaged Brain Tissue

Tapert wanted to find out in what way binge drinking affects a teen's developing brain. So using brain imaging, she focused on the white matter, or nerve tissue, of the brain. "White matter is very important for the relay of information between brain cells; and we know that it is continuing to develop during adolescence," Tapert says.

So Tapert imaged the brains of two groups of high school students: binge drinkers and a matched group of teens with no history of binge drinking. She reports in her recent study a marked difference in the white matter of the binge drinkers. "They appeared to have a number of little dings throughout their brains' white matter, indicating poor quality," Tapert says. And poor quality of the brain's white matter indicates poor, inefficient communication between brain cells.

"These results were actually surprising to me because the binge drinking kids hadn't, in fact, engaged in a great deal of binge drinking. They were drinking on average once or twice a month, but when they did drink, it was to a relatively high quantity of at least four or five drinks an occasion," she says.

In another study, Tapert reported abnormal functioning in the hippocampus—a key area for memory formation—in teen binge drinkers. Reflecting their abnormal brain scans, the teen drinkers did more poorly on learning verbal material than their non-drinking counterparts. What remains unknown, says Tapert, is if the cognitive downward slide in teenage binge drinkers is reversible.

# TEN

# Parents Should Let Teens Drink at Home So They Learn to Drink Responsibly

**Gretchen Anderson**

Gretchen Anderson is a food and wine critic. In the following viewpoint she discusses why she lets her children drink with her. When alcohol is presented as a cultural part of family, friendship, and celebration, she contends, young adults are more likely to enjoy it responsibly and maturely. But when alcohol is forbidden and glorified, young people become so desperate to try it that they do so without respect or caution. Anderson believes that easing children into alcohol use will help them develop a positive and healthy relationship with it. She thinks parents should drink with their children in order to teach them how to enjoy alcohol conscientiously.

We sit down to dinner with friends. I've tossed a spinach salad with dried cherries, blue cheese and balsamic vinegar, and baked homemade rolls to go with the grilled New York strips and bittersweet chocolate mousse. We've already passed around champagne glasses brimming with a sparkling California rosé while snacking on artichoke appetizers, but I smell trouble when Amy declines hers as if she's been offered a rotting carcass by the dog instead of a 91-point bubbly brimming with strawberries and sunshine.

## "Can I Try It?"

At the table, my husband opens a Zinfandel I brought back from a trip to Lodi, California. The wine's deep fruitiness will, I'm sure, please even the apparently unrefined palates of our friends.

"No, thank you." Amy turns her head again as if my husband were passing her a *Playboy* opened to the centerfold. He hesitates, then sets the glass down in the middle of the table, thinking she might change her mind. "I just don't like alcohol," she says, wrinkling her nose. "It's just a personal preference."

"Mom, can I try it?" One of her middle school-age boys looks hopefully at the wine.

"*No.*" She is adamant and horrified.

Is she worried we might think she is a bad mother if she says yes? Or is she against allowing her kids to sample alcohol?

"He's welcome to have a sip as far as we're concerned," I say, playing the good hostess.

The boy brightens. "Please, mom?"

"*No.*" She saws at her steak with a vengeance.

I'm embarrassed, because I gave my five-year-old, Kate, a taste of my bubbly in the kitchen as Amy and I stood chatting. I wonder if Amy is thinking of going straight home and calling Social Services. We do live in the Bible Belt, after all, where the joke is that Jews don't recognize the Messiah, Protestants don't recognize the Pope, and Baptists don't recognize each other in the liquor store.

## Teaching the Joy of Moderation

Nationwide, Americans succumb to extremes, and to excess. We weigh the spectrum from morbidly obese to morbidly anorexic. We eat fast food every day, or only locally-grown, organic fare. We binge drink, or we abstain altogether.

Our country has a stormy history with alcoholic beverages, from the saloons of the Wild West to the bootlegging of Prohibition. Even now, the tenuous post-Prohibition ceasefire still harbors a deep-seated horror of alcohol in general (witness the absurd blue laws), and a special fear of exposing our children to alcohol.

This self-righteous attitude is a touchy trigger for adolescent binge-drinking. Throughout history, children have been inexplicably drawn to the forbidden. When they hear all their lives (while we're feeding them Oreos, Goldfish, and hot dogs) that alcohol is one of the very worst things you can put into your system, they quite naturally want to try it out for themselves. According to the U.S. Substance Abuse and Mental Health Services Organization, 10.1 million twelve-to-twenty-year-olds use alcohol, and almost half of those binge-drink.

In another recent report on binge drinking, British psychology professor Adrian Furnham suggests that parents play the central and the most powerful role in establishing drinking patterns in their children. Parents usually plant their feet firmly in one camp or another, either forbidding alcohol altogether and preaching its perniciousness, or throwing parties in their own home for teenagers, figuring they're going to drink anyway, so let's not let them drive.

I have chosen a different path for my kids, one that winds through center camp.

## Alcohol Is Part of Culture

I write about food and wine for a living. Because of my work, I know a glass a day for a woman, and two glasses for a man, is considered a healthy amount that helps ward off heart disease and a host of other health problems. Because of my work, I also regard wine as a food, as generations of Europeans have done. And I see it as best enjoyed at the table as a complement to the meal.

When five o'clock rolls around, I pour a Vouvray to sip while chopping ingredients for supper. Since they were tiny, our chil-

*The author says children should be encouraged to develop a positive and healthy relationship with alcohol and that parents should drink with their children to teach them to consume alcohol responsibly.*

dren have watched their parents enjoy a mealtime glass, and even taken sips for themselves as we teach them the difference between Prosecco and Champagne, Pinot Grigio and Pinot Noir. (Sophia is partial to reds, I'm proud to note, and both girls love to clink glasses together in a "cheers" and to try to master the swirl of liquid around the glass.)

I may be a renegade in the United States, but many European parents share my philosophy. In France and Italy, most notably, children are brought up in a food-and-wine culture, taught to appreciate the pleasures of the table in many forms. The French writer Colette wrote in *Earthly Paradise*:

> At an age when I could still scarcely read, I was spelling out, drop by drop, old light clarets and dazzling Yquems. Champagne appeared in its turn, a murmur of foam, leaping pearls of air providing an accompaniment to Birthday and First Communion banquets . . . Good lessons, from which I graduated to a familiar and discreet use of wine, not gulped down greedily but measured out into narrow glasses, assimilated mouthful by spaced out meditative mouthful.

Colette captures the key to growing up with wine: in moderation. Just as my five-year-old understands that an occasional cookie is fine for a treat but an entire package in one sitting is not, she also understands that a glass of wine (or in her case, a taste) is a present to be unwrapped slowly and with savor, not an excuse to binge.

## It Is Possible to Find a Balance

In choosing the middle path between teetotalers and heavy drinkers, I walk a fine line. By making the choice to expose my children early on to the pleasures of drinking wine with meals, I'm making the commitment to lead by example, to walk that line of wine-as-a-food and not cross it.

When I was a teenager and a curious cook, I once sampled my mother's sherry, hidden away in the top cupboard above the stove. It was cooking sherry, cheap and salty, and years of absorbing the heat of the stove hadn't improved it one bit. When caught, I was duly punished. Like my friend Amy, my mother didn't believe in children drinking, so I satisfied my curiosity in secret.

It's true that I'm addicted to wine: its culture, science, philosophy. I compulsively seek out the variety, the vintage, the vintner. The

## Some Parents Drink with Their Children to Teach Them Good Habits

A study by a British travel agency found that nearly a quarter of British parents let their children try alcohol while on vacation, even if they are underage. Of parents who let their kids try alcohol, about half said their children were fourteen to fifteen years old.

**Question: "How old was your child when you first let him or her drink underage while on vacation?"**

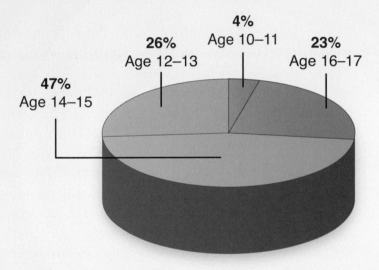

Taken from: "Quarter of Parents Let Underage Kids Drink Alcohol on Holiday." PRLog.com, June 22, 2011.

nuances of the bottle are endlessly fascinating to me, and I hope to impart some of that pleasure onto my kids, just as I hope to instill other precious values into their characters. So I raise my glass to the pleasure of wine: wine at the table, wine as a food, and wine as a family.

# ELEVEN

# Parents Should Not Let Teens Drink at Home

Linda Carroll

Letting children drink with adults is a flawed strategy for preventing underage alcohol abuse reports Linda Carroll in the following viewpoint. Carroll discusses how some people believe that letting teens drink at home, such as is the style in Europe, can help teens develop a mature, responsible relationship with alcohol. But Carroll presents a study that found that teens who drink under adult supervision are more likely to develop problems with alcohol later in life. Teenagers are not merely shorter, thinner adults, argues Carroll—their brains are not finished developing, and they have not yet achieved the maturity to handle a mind-altering drug like alcohol. She concludes that parents who let teens drink at home do them a grave disservice.

Carroll is a contributor to MSNBC.com, which originally published this viewpoint.

As prom night approaches and parents begin to worry about what might happen during after-hour parties, some might be tempted to try to teach their high schoolers to drink responsibly—by allowing them to consume alcohol under supervision.

That approach, scientists now say, is dead wrong.

## Adult Approval Leads to Problems

A new study shows that teens who drink with an adult supervising are more likely to develop problems with alcohol than kids who aren't allowed to touch the stuff till they hit age 21. "The study makes it clear that you shouldn't be drinking with your kids," said Barbara J. McMorris, lead author and a senior research associate at the School of Nursing at the University of Minnesota.

An American Medical Association study reported in 2005 that 25 percent of teens acknowledged they had been at a party where underage drinking was occurring in the presence of a parent. Those are the parents McMorris and her colleagues are hoping the study will reach and teach. For the new study, she and her colleagues rounded up 1,945 seventh graders and then tracked them for three years. Half of the teens were from Victoria, Australia, the other half from Washington State.

## Drinking with Adults Harms Kids

Each year the kids were given questionnaires that asked about their experiences with alcohol and about their relationships with their parents. The teens were asked how often they'd consumed more than a few sips of any alcoholic beverage each time they were surveyed.

When they hit the eighth grade, the teens were asked how many times in the past year they'd consumed alcohol "at dinner, or on a special occasion or holiday, with adult supervision" or "at parties with adult supervision." Researchers didn't specifically ask teens if the adults were drinking with them or were just present. They were also asked how many times they'd experienced harmful consequences, such as "not able to stop once you had started," "became violent and got into fight," "got injured or had an accident," "got so drunk you were sick or passed out," "had sex with someone you later regretted," or "were unable to remember the night before because you had been drinking."

Australian teens were more likely than their American counterparts to be drinking with adult supervision by eighth grade—66 percent versus 35 percent—and they were more likely to have experienced harmful consequences from their drinking—36 percent compared to 21 percent.

## A Strategy That Backfires

No matter which continent kids and parents came from, it was clear that the strategy to teach teens responsible drinking habits through supervised consumption was backfiring.

That finding didn't surprise the experts. "I think the study says something pretty important," said Patrick Tolan, director of Youth-Nex: The University of Virginia Center to Promote Effective Youth Development. "Parents need to make it clear that it's not OK for kids to drink until they reach the legal drinking age—a line has to be drawn."

Still, many parents seem to have a particularly difficult time drawing lines when it comes to alcohol, said Mary O'Connor, a professor in the department of psychiatry and biobehavioral sciences at the University of California–Los Angeles. "There are people I know who are very responsible parents in many ways who think that this is part of being a responsible parent," O'Connor said. That may be related to our own mixed feelings about a substance that is actually a legal, mind-altering drug.

## Teens Are Not Just Small Adults

What parents tend to forget is that teens are not just smaller versions of us. Their brains have not finished developing, and studies have shown that alcohol has a very different effect on the unfinished brain, O'Connor said. "We know from both animal and human studies that alcohol affects brain development," O'Connor said. "The teenage brain is much more vulnerable to begin with and we now know that repeated drinking can lead to long term deficits in learning and memory."

Beyond this, there's mounting data showing that it can be dangerous to start drinking young, said Dr. Brian Primack, an assistant professor of medicine and pediatrics at the University of Pittsburgh Medical Center. Studies have shown that kids are

# Most Teens Drink at Home or at Someone Else's Home

Underage binge drinking is most likely to occur in private residences. There is debate over whether allowing teens to drink at a person's home offers them a safe environment in which to experiment or puts them at risk for several alcohol-related problems.

## Drinking Locations by Age Group

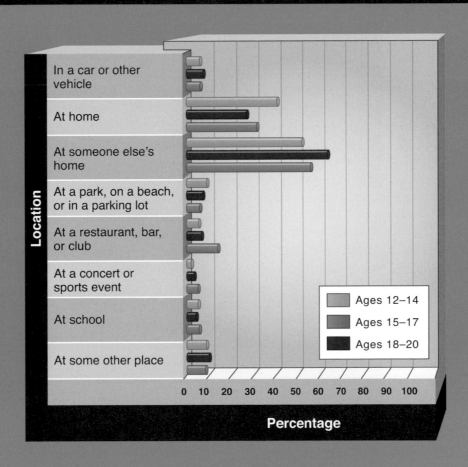

Taken from: *Report to Congress on the Prevention and Reduction of Underage Drinking.* Department of Health and Human Service, Substance Abuse and Mental Health Services Administration (SAMHSA), May 2011, p. 12. http://store.samhas.gov/shin/content/SMA11-4645/SMA11-4645.pdf.

four times more likely to become alcoholics if they start drinking before age 15, Primack said. So, is it enough to simply draw the line and tell your kids they can't touch a drop till they're 21? Will that glass of wine with dinner—made all the more necessary by rebellious teens you live with—encourage them to drink too much? Not necessarily, experts say.

*Studies have shown that kids are four times more likely to become alcoholics if they start drinking before age fifteen.*

## Parents Should Model Moderation

"You want to model moderation," Tolan explained. "You don't want to be drinking a lot in front of them—or inviting them to parties where your friends will be drinking a lot. That will confuse them and lead them to think that it's OK to drink a lot." You don't have to lock down the liquor cabinet, he added, but "that said, you should remember that kids experiment."

Parents should know know exactly what and how much alcohol they've got, O'Connor said. "And you want to taste it periodically to make sure it's not been diluted," she added. That's well and good for when your kids are at home. But what about that prom night situation? The solution might be a simple one—let your teen host the party at your house. "I think alcohol free parties are a great idea," McMorris said.

# TWELVE

# Banning Caffeinated Alcohol Drinks Can Reduce Underage Binge Drinking

**Robyn Schelenz**

In the following viewpoint Robyn Schelenz argues that alcoholic beverages that contain caffeine should be banned. Schelenz explains that drinks like Four Loko, which was withdrawn from shelves in 2010 but reintroduced back into the market without some of the original ingredients, are dangerous because they contain much greater concentrations of alcohol and caffeine than traditional cocktails, such as rum and colas or Irish coffees. When consumed by young people, who are inexperienced at handling any amount of alcohol, Four Loko becomes a toxic, potentially deadly drink. Schelenz applauds the government's decision to take action against the so-called energy drink and supports laws that restrict the extent to which alcohol products can be marketed to young people.

Schelenz is a blogger for Home Health Testing and contributes articles to Food Safety News, the website that originally published this viewpoint.

As of last week [in November 2010], the popular alcoholic energy drink Four Loko has met its demise. The Food and Drug Administration [FDA] sent a letter on Nov. 17 to manufacturers of alcoholic energy drinks stating that they found the combination of caffeine and alcohol in these drinks to be "unsafe." Not a surprising outcome when you consider the recent bans of the 12 percent ABV [alcohol by volume] energy drink in states like Washington and New York.

*The author says caffeinated alcoholic drinks like these are dangerous because they contain greater concentrations of alcohol and caffeine than traditional cocktails.*

# How Safe Is Alcohol Mixed with Caffeine?

Although the crackdown comes much to the delight of college administrators struggling to deal with a Four Loko–related mayhem, for others it has provoked accusations about the "nanny state" and FDA hypocrisy. Much of the outcry echoes what

## Caffeine, Alcohol, and Blood Alcohol Concentration (BAC)

BAC (blood alcohol concentration) is a measure of how much alcohol is in one's blood. The table below offers an estimated BAC level if one were to consume one caffeinated alcoholic drink within an hour.

| Weight (in lbs.) | BAC After Consumption of a 23.5-ounce Caffeinated Alcoholic Beverage in One Hour | | | |
|---|---|---|---|---|
| | 12% alcohol/volume | | 9.9% alcohol/volume | |
| | Female | Male | Male | Female |
| 100 | 0.24 | 0.19 | 0.19 | 0.16 |
| 110 | 0.22 | 0.19 | 0.19 | 0.14 |
| 120 | 0.20 | 0.16 | 0.16 | 0.13 |
| 130 | 0.18 | 0.15 | 0.15 | 0.12 |
| 140 | 0.17 | 0.14 | 0.14 | 0.11 |
| 150 | 0.16 | 0.13 | 0.13 | 0.10 |
| 160 | 0.15 | 0.12 | 0.12 | 0.09 |
| 170 | 0.14 | 0.11 | 0.11 | 0.09 |
| 180 | 0.13 | 0.10 | 0.10 | 0.08 |
| 190 | 0.12 | 0.10 | 0.10 | 0.08 |
| 200 | 0.12 | 0.09 | 0.09 | 0.07 |
| 210 | 0.11 | 0.09 | 0.09 | 0.07 |
| 220 | 0.10 | 0.08 | 0.08 | 0.07 |
| 230 | 0.10 | 0.08 | 0.08 | 0.06 |
| 240 | 0.09 | 0.07 | 0.08 | 0.06 |
| 250 | 0.09 | 0.07 | 0.07 | 0.06 |

Taken from: "Put Some Think Behind Your Drink." New York State College Health Association, 2011.

Phusion Projects wrote in its own defense, in a Nov. 16 [2010] statement about eliminating caffeine in their product:

> We have repeatedly contended—and still believe, as do many people throughout the country—that the combination of alcohol and caffeine is safe. If it were unsafe, popular drinks like rum and colas or Irish coffees that have been consumed safely and responsibly for years would face the same scrutiny that our products have recently faced.

Phusion Projects is correct—many people do feel the combination of alcohol and caffeine is safe. The company's mistake is in conflating drinks like Irish coffees with its own product.

## The Problem Is Quantity and Volume

The main issue with Four Loko is not that it simply combines caffeine and alcohol, but that it does so in massive quantities. Take, for example, a recipe for a rum and coke—5 oz. of cola and 1.5 oz. of rum. This is a fairly typical size and contains roughly 14.5 mg of caffeine and 0.6 oz. of alcohol, assuming the rum is 40 percent ABV.

Or take a sample recipe for Irish coffee, containing 6 oz. of coffee, 1.5 oz. of whiskey, a teaspoon of brown sugar and cream. Assuming the whiskey is 40 percent ABV, your drink will have something like 90 mg of caffeine and 0.6 oz. of alcohol. Now take Four Loko—a 23.5 oz. can at 12 percent ABV has 156 mg of caffeine and 2.82 oz. of alcohol.

To get a "Four Loko effect" with a rum and coke you'd have to drink 4.7 rum and cokes. This would have the same alcohol content as a Four Loko, but you'd lack the caffeine. At only 68.15 mg, it's less than half the caffeine in a Four Loko.

## Multiple Drinks in One

To equal a Four Loko with an Irish coffee, you'd only have to drink a little less than two Irish coffees. That's in the caffeine department anyway. To truly equal a Four Loko you would have to pour at least twice as much whiskey into each serving. If that sounds like a strong and probably unappetizing drink, that's because it is.

Note that to achieve Four Loko–like effects with these drinks you'd have to consume more than one serving of each drink. With Four Loko all you need is one can. Consider, too, that Four Loko is a carbonated beverage, so if it's not finished in one sitting, it will go flat. It's all the more encouragement to consume the whole thing and go overboard in mixing caffeine and alcohol. The comparisons then, between Four Loko and mixed drinks do not hold up, regardless of what Phusion Projects and its fans say.

## An Excessive Product

Caffeine and alcohol won't send you to the emergency room when used in moderation, but Four Loko is far from moderate. Consumers should have the right to combine caffeine and alcohol if they so choose, but Four Loko does so at levels that are excessive and in the words of the FDA, "unsafe."

# THIRTEEN

# Banning Caffeinated Alcohol Drinks Will Not Reduce Underage Binge Drinking

**Jacob Sullum**

> Banning caffeinated alcohol drinks is not the right way to reduce underage binge drinking, argues Jacob Sullum in the following viewpoint. Sullum discusses the controversy over a caffeinated alcoholic beverage called Four Loko, which was marketed as an alcoholic energy drink until it was withdrawn in 2010 (it has since reappeared on the market, minus some of the more controversial ingredients). Four Loko was never as dangerous or concentrated as its opponents made it out to be, argues Sullum. He says politicians and newspapers that made such a fuss over the drink are guilty of spreading unwarranted panic and hysteria. Sullum says that even if Four Loko and drinks like it are banned, teenagers will find a way to mix caffeine with alcohol.
>
> Sullum is a senior editor at *Reason*, a libertarian magazine published by the Reason Foundation.

Timothy Leary [1960s Harvard psychology professor and LSD guru] noted that "psychedelic drugs cause panic and temporary insanity" in people who have never tried them. The same can be said of Four Loko, the drink that federal regulators banned last week [in November 2010] amid a nationwide fit of hysteria about "a toxic, dangerous mix of caffeine and alcohol" that Sen. Charles Schumer (D-N.Y.) warned was "spreading like a plague across the country." A fruity, bubbly, neon-colored plague.

## Government Fear-Mongering

The main knock against Four Loko, which is less potent than Chardonnay, is that the caffeine masks the alcohol's effects, leading people to underestimate their impairment and drink more than they otherwise would. Two studies have found that college students who drink alcohol combined with caffeine tend to consume more and take more risks than college students who drink alcohol by itself.

Neither study clarified whether the difference was due to the caffeine or to the pre-existing tendencies of hard partiers who are attracted to drinks they believe will help keep them going all night long. But that distinction did not matter to panic-promoting politicians and their publicists in the press, who breathlessly advertised Four Loko while marveling at its rising popularity. Like other officially condemned intoxicants, Four Loko was linked to a disfavored group—reckless, hedonistic "young people"—and everything about it was viewed in that light.

Over and over again, fear-mongering officials and hyperbolic reporters cited two incidents—one at Ramapo College in New Jersey, the other at Central Washington University—in which students who drank Four Loko were taken to the hospital. These 15 students, most of whom seem to have been drinking other alcoholic beverages in addition to Four Loko, represent something like 0.015 percent of the 100,000 or so 18-to-20-year-olds who make alcohol-related visits to American emergency rooms each year. Yet their drunken stupidity was repeatedly presented as evidence of Four Loko's unique dangers.

# Caffeinated Alcoholic Beverages: High Calories, Mixed Alcohol

The following chart contains information about caffeinated alcoholic beverages.*

| Product | Supplier | Ingredients | Alcohol Content | Container Size | Estimated Calories | Estimated Number of Standard Drinks |
|---|---|---|---|---|---|---|
| 808 | Liquid Arts Beverage Group | Cognac, vodka, liquor, caffeine, and guarana | 10% | 12 oz. | 350 | 2 |
| Axis | Associated Brewing Company | Artificial flavors, wormwood oil, and certified color | 12% | 16 oz. | 400 | 3.2 |
| BE | Anheuser-Busch Inc. | Beer, caffeine, ginseng, and guarana extract | 6.60% | 10 oz. | 250 | 1.1 |
| California Organic Brewery, MateVeza | Rave Associates, Inc. | Beer with Yerba mate (caffeinated tea) | 5% | 22 oz. | 500 | 1.8 |
| Carpe Noctum A.M. | Atomic Brands, Inc. | Vodka, caffeine, taurine, natural and artificial flavors | 9% | 12.68 oz. | 350 | 1.9 |
| Core | Associated Brewing Company | Artificial flavors, wormwood oil, color | 12% | 23.5 oz. | 700 | 4.8 |
| Core | Associated Brewing Company | Malt beverages with natural and artificial flavors, taurine, guarana, ginseng, caffeine | 12% | 23.5 oz. | 700 | 4.8 |
| Four Loko Beverages | Phusion Projects, LLC | Malt beverage with natural and artificial flavors, taurine, guarana, ginseng, caffeine | 12% | 23.5 oz. | 700 | 4.8 |
| Jack Daniel's Country Cocktail, Black Jack Cola | Brown-Forman Corporation | Malt beverage with natural flavors, artificial color, and caffeine | 5% | 10 oz. | 200 | .08 |
| Joose, Max | United Brands Company, Inc. | Malt beverage with natural flavors, ginseng, taurine, caffeine | 12% | 23.5 oz. | 700 | 4.8 |
| Joose Mamba, Joose Orange, Panther Joose | United Brands Company, Inc. | Malt beverage with natural flavors, caffeine, ginseng, taurine, and certified colors | 9.90% | 23.5–24 oz. | 700 | 5 |

*Note: Since the creation of this document, some of these beverages are no longer in production.

Taken from: Jessica Greber and Sara Stahlman. "Alcohol Mixed with High Levels of Caffeine: What Campus Professionals Need to Know." College Student Educators International, 2010, p. 6.

## Panic and Hysteria

Likewise, the National Highway Traffic Safety Administration counted 13,800 alcohol-related fatalities in 2008. It did not put crashes involving Four Loko drinkers in a special category. But news organizations around the country, primed to perceive the drink as unusually hazardous, routinely do. Three days before the Food and Drug Administration [FDA] declared Four Loko illegal, a 14-year-old stole his parents' SUV and crashed it into a guard rail in Denton, Texas, killing his girlfriend. Here is how the local

*US senator Charles Schumer speaks at a news conference on November 10, 2010, to call upon the state of New York to ban sales of caffeinated alcoholic beverages. He claimed such drinks were "spreading like a plague across the country."*

Fox station headlined its story: "'Four Loko' Found in Deadly Teen Crash."

Connecticut Attorney General Richard Blumenthal (who will soon join Schumer in the Senate) calls Four Loko a "witch's brew," and apparently it really does have magical powers. Although one 23.5-ounce container has less alcohol than a bottle of wine, news reports call it "blackout in a can." ABC News implies that a single can, containing as much caffeine as a cup of coffee, can trigger a fatal heart attack in a perfectly healthy person.

*The New York Times* reports that Four Loko, which features a drug combination familiar to fans of Irish coffee or rum and cola, "has been blamed" for causing a 20-year-old Florida college student to shoot himself in the head. A CBS station in Philadelphia said a middle-aged suburban dad suffered "a hallucinogenic frenzy" featuring "nightmarish delusions" after a can and a half, while another CBS affiliate in Baltimore said two cans made a 20-year-old "lose her mind," steal a friend's pickup truck, and crash it into a telephone pole. Under the evil influence of this demonic drink, the *St. Petersburg Times* reports, a 21-year-old in New Port Richey, Florida, broke into an old woman's house, trashed the place, stripped naked, and took a dump on the floor.

## Teens Will Drink What They Want

Despite such alarming reports, the FDA did not conclude that alcoholic beverages containing caffeine, which are made by dozens of companies, are inherently unsafe. Instead it focused on Four Loko's manufacturer and three other companies that "seemingly target the young adult user," who is "especially vulnerable" to "combined ingestion of caffeine and alcohol"—and too dumb, apparently, to mix vodka with Red Bull.

# FOURTEEN

# Single-Sex Dormitories Can Prevent Underage Drinking

## John Garvey

John Garvey is the president of The Catholic University of America in Washington, DC. He explains that as more college and university dorms have become co-ed, binge drinking and casual sex have increased. Binge drinking leads young people toward regrettable experiences, such as anonymous, unsafe sex and potentially fatal drunk driving accidents. It puts students at risk for experiencing unplanned pregnancy, depression, and other problems. In Garvey's opinion, college should be a place of virtue and respect, but underage drinking and its related behaviors encourage neither. He thinks returning to single-sex dormitory living will greatly reduce underage binge drinking and the host of problems that come with it.

My wife and I have sent five children to college and our youngest just graduated. Like many parents, we encouraged them to study hard and spend time in a country where people don't speak English. Like all parents, we worried about the kind of people they would grow up to be.

## College Should Be a Place of Virtue

We may have been a little unusual in thinking it was the college's responsibility to worry about that too. But I believe that intellect and virtue are connected. They influence one another. Some say the intellect is primary. If we know what is good, we will pursue it. Aristotle suggests in the "Nicomachean Ethics" that the influence runs the other way. He says that if you want to listen intelligently to lectures on ethics you "must have been brought up in good habits." The goals we set for ourselves are brought into focus by our moral vision.

"Virtue," Aristotle concludes, "makes us aim at the right mark, and practical wisdom makes us take the right means." If he is right, then colleges and universities should concern themselves with virtue as well as intellect.

I want to mention two places where schools might direct that concern, and a slightly old-fashioned remedy that will improve the practice of virtue. The two most serious ethical challenges college students face are binge drinking and the culture of hooking up.

"THE GOOD NEWS IS, HE GOT A 3.0...THE BAD NEWS IS IT'S HIS BLOOD ALCOHOL COUNT..."

## Results of Binge Drinking

Alcohol-related accidents are the leading cause of death for young adults aged 17–24. Students who engage in binge drinking (about two in five) are 25 times more likely to do things like miss class, fall behind in school work, engage in unplanned sexual activity, and get in trouble with the law. They also cause trouble for other

*In the author's opinion returning to same-sex dormitory living will greatly reduce underage binge drinking and other problems that accompany it.*

students, who are subjected to physical and sexual assault, suffer property damage and interrupted sleep, and end up babysitting problem drinkers.

Hooking up is getting to be as common as drinking. Sociologist W. Bradford Wilcox, who heads the National Marriage Project at the University of Virginia, says that in various studies, 40%–64% of college students report doing it.

The effects are not all fun. Rates of depression reach 20% for young women who have had two or more sexual partners in the last year, almost double the rate for women who have had none. Sexually active young men do more poorly than abstainers in their academic work. And as we have always admonished our own children, sex on these terms is destructive of love and marriage.

## Abandon Co-Ed Housing

Here is one simple step colleges can take to reduce both binge drinking and hooking up: Go back to single-sex residences.

I know it's countercultural. More than 90% of college housing is now co-ed. But Christopher Kaczor at Loyola Marymount points to a surprising number of studies showing that students in co-ed dorms (41.5%) report weekly binge drinking more than twice as often as students in single-sex housing (17.6%). Similarly, students in co-ed housing are more likely (55.7%) than students in single-sex dorms (36.8%) to have had a sexual partner in the last year—and more than twice as likely to have had three or more.

The point about sex is no surprise. The point about drinking is. I would have thought that young women would have a civilizing influence on young men. Yet the causal arrow seems to run the other way. Young women are trying to keep up—and young men are encouraging them (maybe because it facilitates hooking up).

## Help Students Honor Themselves

Next year all freshmen at The Catholic University of America will be assigned to single-sex residence halls. The year after, we will extend the change to the sophomore halls. It will take a few years to complete the transformation.

The change will probably cost more money. There are a few architectural adjustments. We won't be able to let the ratio of men and women we admit into the freshman class vary from year to year with the size and quality of the pools. But our students will be better off.

# FIFTEEN

# Underage Drinkers Should Be Given Medical Amnesty

**Raymond Updyke**

> Raymond Updyke was a student at the University of Maine when he originally wrote the following viewpoint. In it, he advocates taking a harm-reduction approach to binge drinking. Updyke agrees that binge drinking is a serious problem on many college campuses, resulting in hospital visits, accidents, and death. However, Updyke does not agree that punishing underage drinkers with expulsion, jail time, or similarly harsh penalties will do anything to curb the behavior. On the contrary, he thinks harsh punishments prevent young people from seeking medical attention, because they fear getting in trouble. He suggests that minors who get caught binge drinking should be offered "medical amnesty," which would excuse them from punishment if they bring someone to the hospital while drunk. Updyke contends that underage drinking is not going to stop, but harm-reductive policies like medical amnesty can help prevent alcohol-related fatalities nonetheless.

It is rare to find anything of interest in a public speaking class. One persuasive speech, though, got my attention—it dealt with lowering the drinking age back to 18.

The majority of the cases for lowering the drinking age have been struck down throughout the 1990s and 2000s. State Supreme Courts have ruled the change as unconstitutional and most Americans—77 percent in a 2007 Gallup poll—do not want to lower the drinking age.

While most Americans believe the drinking age should stay at 21, one particular issue sticks out in the maintenance of today's drinking age. Binge drinking has been increasing in the United States, according to a 2003 American Medical Association report. College-aged students are no exception.

With this increase in binge drinking, negative effects associated with alcoholic overdose and intoxication become more apparent. That means more hospital visits, reckless acts like drunk

*Although underage binge drinking cannot be completely stopped, harm-reductive policies like medical amnesty can help prevent alcohol-related fatalities, the author argues.*

driving and even alcohol-related deaths. So what? These events have always occurred and will always continue if binge drinking occurs. But there is something missing.

## Stop Punishing Those Who Seek Help

What happens if you drink too much and you need to go the hospital because your life is at risk? What happens if the only person around is a minor who has consumed or possessed alcohol? Here at the University of Maine, we have the Medical Amnesty Initiative. The initiative states that a student's "fear of getting themselves or another person in trouble may inhibit students from seeking assistance for someone who has had too much to drink" and the program strives to "minimize any barriers which might prevent a student from calling for assistance for someone who has had too much to drink." Students who are accepted into this program and are enrolled in an educational program "will not have a university sanction for an alcohol violation under the Student Code of Conduct."

National law does not mandate this. There are numerous different state laws that exempt minors in possession of alcohol from punishment—bartending, family occasions, religious, educational and even on private property. Yet only three states—Colorado, Florida and Montana—exempt minors in possession of alcohol who report medical need for another minor. The state of Maine is not one of these states with a state-wide medical amnesty exemption.

## Medical Amnesty Protects People

Here is my point: People under the age of 21 who overdose on alcohol need medical help. Otherwise they risk serious harm, or even death—plain and simple. A person under the age of 21 should never have to be afraid of legal repercussions from saving the life of a person in serious harm due to alcohol. The current law needs to change so that people under 21 who are in possession of alcohol can be safeguarded when responding to the medical needs of an intoxicated, underage person.

The Medical Amnesty program is a great step in the right direction, yet the state of Maine needs to recognize that people under the age of 21 need to be protected. We should not be punishing underage individuals who try to prevent the death of another person. This may seem like a no-brainer, but no action is being taken.

## A Good Way to Save Lives

It is time for change. The parent who buries their child because their underage friends feared getting caught drinking knows how powerful this exemption is.

In America, we strive for life, liberty and the pursuit of happiness. It is time we take a stand for life. Until then, society as a whole will bury each minor who dies from intoxication because their peers were too afraid of legalities and had to watch their friend die.

Take a shovel and start digging, or stop the fear.

# SIXTEEN

# Underage Drinkers Should Take Alcohol Classes

**John McCardell**

In the following viewpoint John McCardell suggests that teaching underage drinkers about alcohol could curb binge drinking. McCardell admits that the problem of underage drinking is serious—according to him, alcohol-related injuries, accidents, and deaths are on the rise, and underage drinking contributes to sexual assaults, depression, and other serious problems. But in his opinion, the minimum drinking age and similarly restrictive policies have failed to curb this destructive behavior. He thinks a better approach would be to teach young people how to drink responsibly via alcohol classes. McCardell thinks that treating young people like adults will help them handle alcohol like adults, too.

McCardell is the former president of Middlebury College and the founder of the Amethyst Initiative, an organization of college and university presidents who collectively advocate lowering the drinking age to eighteen.

High-school seniors tend to hold romantic notions of college life: newfound freedoms, enlightenment, keg-fueled free-for-alls. But the last attraction has lately achieved a new prominence: at one major university, student visits to the emergency room for alcohol-related treatment have increased by 84 percent in the past three years [2006–2009].

## Underage Drinking Is a Crisis

Between 1993 and 2001, 18-to-20-year-olds showed a 56 percent jump in the rate of heavy-drinking episodes. Underage drinkers

*Graduate student Roberto Vaca poses in front of his alcohol-education class at California State University at Fresno. School officials report a trend toward less alcohol use by students who have taken Vaca's course.*

## Progressive Effects of Alcohol

Blood alcohol concentration (BAC) is a measure of how much alcohol is in a person's bloodstream. Different levels have different effects.

| Blood Alcohol Concentration | Changes in Feelings and Personality | Brain Regions Affected | Impaired Activities (continuum) |
|---|---|---|---|
| 0.01–0.05 | Relaxation, sense of well-being, loss of inhibition | Cerebral cortex | Alertness, judgment |
| 0.06–0.10 | Pleasure, numbness of feelings, nausea, sleepiness, emotional arousal | Cerebral cortex + forebrain | Coordination (especially fine motor skills), visual tracking |
| **\*\*-0.08—legal limit for driving** | | | |
| 0.11–0.20 | Mood swings, anger, sadness, mania | Cerebral cortex + forebrain + cerebellum | Reasoning and depth perception |
| 0.21–0.30 | Aggression, reduced sensations, stupor, depression | Cerebral cortex + forebrain + cerebellum + brain stem | Inappropriate social behavior (e.g., obnoxiousness), slurred speech, lack of balance |
| 0.31–0.40 | Unconsciousness, death possible, coma | Entire brain | Loss of temperature regulation, loss of bladder control, difficulty breathing, slowed heart rate |
| 0.41 and greater | Death | Entire brain | |

Taken from: National Institutes of Health. National Institute on Alcohol Abuse and Alcoholism, 2012.

now consume more than 90 percent of their alcohol during binges. These alarming rates have life-threatening consequences: each year, underage drinking kills some 5,000 young people and contributes to roughly 600,000 injuries and 100,000 cases of sexual assault among college students.

## Solutions to the Problem Have Failed

The way our society addresses this problem has been about as effective as a parachute that opens on the second bounce. Clearly, state laws mandating a minimum drinking age of 21 haven't eliminated drinking by young adults—they've simply driven it underground, where life and health are at greater risk. Merely adjusting the legal age up or down doesn't work—we've tried that already and failed. But federal law has stifled the ability to conceive of more creative solutions in the only place where the Constitution says such debate should happen—in the state house—because any state that sets its drinking age lower than 21 forfeits 10 percent of its federal highway funds. This is called an "incentive."

## Teach Alcohol, Do Not Hide It

So what might states, freed from this federal penalty, do differently? They might license 18-year-olds—adults in the eyes of the law—to drink, provided they've completed high school, attended an alcohol-education course (that consists of more than temperance lectures and scare tactics), and kept a clean record. They might even mandate alcohol education at a young age. And they might also adopt zero-tolerance laws for drunk drivers of all ages, and require ignition interlocks on their cars. Such initiatives, modeled on driver's education, might finally reverse the trend of consumption by young people at ever earlier ages. Binge drinking is as serious a crisis today as drunk driving was two decades ago. It's time we tackled the problem like adults.

# What You Should Know About Underage Drinking

## Facts About Underage Drinkers

Each year, the National Institute on Drug Abuse of the National Institutes of Health publishes the Monitoring the Future Study, which surveys drug and alcohol trends among America's youth. The 2011 version of the study reported that

- 33 percent of current eighth graders have tried alcohol;
- 56 percent of tenth graders have tried alcohol;
- 70 percent of twelfth graders have tried alcohol;
- 81 percent of college students have tried alcohol;
- 87 percent of young adults (nineteen to twenty-eight years old) have tried alcohol;
- 6 percent of eighth graders reported drinking five or more drinks in a row (binge drinking) in the past 2 weeks;
- 15 percent of tenth graders reported binge drinking in the past 2 weeks;
- 22 percent of twelfth graders reported binge drinking in the past 2 weeks;
- 36 percent of college students reported binge drinking in the past 2 weeks;
- 37 percent of young adults reported binge drinking in the past 2 weeks;
- 26 percent of twelfth-grade males reported binge drinking in the previous 2 weeks;

- 18 percent of twelfth-grade females reported binge drinking in the previous 2 weeks;
- 43 percent of college males reported binge drinking in the previous 2 weeks; and
- 32 percent of college females reported binge drinking in the previous 2 weeks.

The Underage Drinking Enforcement Training Center reports that in the United States in 2009
- more than 12 million underage drinkers consume alcohol each year;
- 72.5 percent of high school students have had at least one drink of alcohol on one or more days during their life;
- 21 percent of high school students drank alcohol (beyond a few sips) before age thirteen;
- 42 percent of high school students had at least one drink of alcohol one or more times in the past thirty days;
- 24 percent of high school students binge drank (had five or more drinks of alcohol in a row) in the past thirty days;
- 4.5 percent of high school students had at least one drink of alcohol on school property in the past thirty days; and
- underage customers consumed 16.2 percent of all alcohol sold in the United States.

According to the Substance Abuse and Mental Health Services Administration (SAMHSA),
- 6 percent of adolescents aged twelve to fourteen drank alcohol in the past month;
- 93.4 percent received their alcohol for free the last time they drank;
- about 317,000 (44.8 percent) twelve- to fourteen-year-olds who drank in the past month received their alcohol for free from their family or at home;
- about 15.7 percent (or an estimated 111,000) were provided alcohol for free by their parents or guardians.

According to the Centers for Disease Control and Prevention,

- alcohol is the most commonly used and abused drug among youth in the United States, more than tobacco and illicit drugs;
- people aged twelve to twenty consume 11 percent of all alcohol in the United States;
- more than 90 percent of this alcohol is consumed via binge drinking;
- in 2008 there were approximately 190,000 emergency rooms visits by persons under age twenty-one for injuries and other conditions linked to alcohol;
- 10 percent of high school students reported driving after drinking alcohol within the past month; and
- 28 percent of high school students reported riding with a driver who had been drinking alcohol within the past month.

## Facts About Why Teens Choose Not to Drink

The Century Council reported on a study that surveyed teens' reasons for not drinking. Among them were that

- 66 percent said they "don't want to";
- 62 percent said "it is unsafe/unhealthy";
- 57 percent said "because it is illegal";
- 54 percent said "parents asked/told me not to"; and
- 49 percent said "because it is not cool."

The Century Council also reported on a study that asked kids what punishments or threats might prevent them from drinking, and

- 68 percent said the threat of getting in trouble with the police/law;
- 55 percent said the threat of getting in trouble at or suspended from school;
- 44 percent said suspended or kicked off a team or club;
- 42 percent said getting grounded;
- 42 percent said losing computer/Internet/IM privileges;
- 41 percent said getting kicked out of the house;

- 37 percent said getting yelled at;
- 33 percent said losing their allowance; and
- 32 percent said losing their driving privileges.

The GfK Roper Youth Report asked youth who had the most influence on whether or not they drank. Students could give multiple answers, which included:
- their parents (83 percent);
- their friends (33 percent);
- their teachers (33 percent);
- their siblings (24 percent);
- the media (12 percent); and
- ads/television (10 percent).

## American Opinions About Underage Drinking

A 2009 poll by CBS News asked Americans whether they would approve or disapprove of states' lowering the drinking age to eighteen if states felt it would give the police more time to enforce other laws. The poll found that
- 24 percent would approve;
- 73 percent would disapprove; and
- 3 percent were unsure.

A 2007 Gallup poll asked Americans about their attitudes toward the drinking age and found that
- 22 percent would favor a federal law that would lower the drinking age in all states to eighteen;
- 77 would oppose such a law;
- 1 percent were unsure;
- 60 percent said the penalties for underage drinking should be more strict;
- 6 percent said penalties should be less strict;
- 31 percent said they should remain as they are; and
- 3 percent were unsure.

# What You Should Do About Underage Drinking

Underage drinking is probably something you have encountered or will at some point. The following information can help you decide how to deal with the issue.

## Reasons to Turn Down Alcohol

Teens who drink are at serious risk of dying or getting hurt in a car accident. In 2011 the Underage Drinking Enforcement Training Center (UDETC) reported that 1,506 underage drinkers were killed in traffic accidents in 2009, and another 36,000 people were injured in car accidents that were caused by underage drinking. Teens who drink are prone to making other bad decisions. In 2007, for example, underage drinking was a contributing factor in 359 fatal burns, drownings, and suicides. Most teens view themselves as immortal, and many think such tragedies are not likely to happen to them. Remember that the teens who died or were hurt in such accidents likely viewed themselves the same way.

Alcohol also fuels regrettable, risky, or otherwise negative sexual experiences for teens. For example, the UDETC reports that in 2009, more than 28,000 teen pregnancies were attributable to underage drinking. Another 937,000 teens had risky or unprotected sex, putting them at high risk for sexually transmitted diseases, pregnancy, and mental and social anguish. Information provided by the National Institute on Alcohol Abuse and Alcoholism and the federal government further adds to this grim picture: In one year, 97,000 students between the ages of eighteen and twenty-four reported being victims of alcohol-related sexual assault or date rape. Another 400,000 reported having unprotected sex while drunk, and 100,000 reported being too drunk to remember whether they had consented to sex or whether they had used protection. The sexual experiences you have as a young person will shape your personality and relationships for the rest of your life, so it is important to make smart, healthy decisions in this area early on.

Aside from physical harm, drinking beyond your limits puts you at risk of embarrassing yourself in ways that might be talked about for years to come. People who drink lose their inhibitions and control of themselves, and from this compromised state, they may act stupidly in ways they will deeply regret. Every high school student body has the person who drank too much and did or said things he or she was later embarrassed about. Such incidents no longer die within days or weeks of a party; embarrassing, compromising photos posted to the Internet or texted around groups of friends haunt forever. Staying in control of yourself at all times greatly reduces your chances of becoming a cautionary tale, a sob story, the butt of jokes, or worse.

## Ways to Turn Down Alcohol

Turning down alcohol is easier than people think, and there are lots of different ways to do so. The simplest, and classic, way is to just say no, with confidence and surety. When you approach your choices with confidence, people surprisingly respect them. If you are at a party and are offered alcohol, simply say, "No thanks" with your head held high. Even though your peers may not say so openly, many of them will respect your confidence and marvel at your ability to stand up to peer pressure; they may even wish the same for themselves. You might even become someone who sets an example for others, which is a powerful feeling. If saying no feels too harsh, you can say, "I'm good right now, thanks," thus putting the issue off until others find something else to focus on. You can also volunteer to be the designated driver, which is a good reason for people to accept your decision to turn down drinking.

If bluntly turning down alcohol feels a little too difficult, there are a couple of excuses you could use to back you up. You can let people know you are taking a medication that cannot be mixed with alcohol—several types of antibiotics, skin medications, antidepressants, and other medications are not safe to mix with alcohol. Simply tell people you are finishing up a course of amoxicillin and do not want alcohol to undermine the medicine's effectiveness. You can also tell people you are allergic to alcohol—a common reaction to alcohol that includes flushed cheeks, congested nose, itchy eyes, sneezing, headache, and nausea.

You might feel like you need to go into further detail about why you do not want to drink, and that's OK—there are plenty of legitimate reasons to offer. If you are athletic, you can say, "I've been working out, and alcohol really messes with my performance." You can let people know that alcohol actually interferes with the body's ability to build muscle—it slows down protein synthesis and contributes to dehydration, both of which undo the hard training undertaken by student athletes. In addition to undermining your athletic training, it is very possible that you have a game or practice the next morning, and you can just let people know it is not worth it to you to be hung over, or that you would not feel right letting down your team like that.

Similarly, if you are watching your weight, simply let people know that alcohol's extra calories are not worth it to you. In truth, alcohol is packed with calories: One beer has between 100 and 200 calories, and is also chock full of carbohydrates. Just one shot of vodka has more than 60 calories, and the calorie count of a drink climbs when mixed with juice or soda. Having just two or three drinks, therefore, can add between 500 and 600 calories to your daily intake—the equivalent of about three glazed donuts or a large order of french fries! Just let people know that alcohol's empty calories do not go with your goal of looking hot.

Finally, you can carry a "decoy" drink, if it makes you feel too uncomfortable to announce that you are abstaining from alcohol. In the same kind of cup that others are using for drinks, pour yourself tonic water, juice, iced tea, or a soft drink. Garnish with a lemon wedge or a straw. Sip slowly and no one will know, or care, what is in your cup.

Remember that you have the rest of your life to enjoy alcohol responsibly. Realize that underage drinking is typically accompanied by more problems than benefits. Kids who drink usually do so for the wrong reasons and often regret their drunken behavior. Sometimes, they even pay with their lives. Approach alcohol the way in which you approach all of life's other challenges and obstacles: with confidence, responsibility, and intelligence.

# ORGANIZATIONS TO CONTACT

The editors have compiled the following list of organizations concerned with the issues debated in this book. The descriptions are derived from materials provided by the organizations. All have publications or information available for interested readers. The list was compiled on the date of publication of the present volume; names, addresses, phone and fax numbers, and e-mail and Internet addresses may change. Be aware that many organizations take several weeks or longer to respond to inquiries, so allow as much time as possible.

**Al-Anon/AlaTeen**
1600 Corporate Landing Pkwy.
Virginia Beach, VA 23454
(757) 563-1600
e-mail: wso@al-anon.org
website: www.al-anon.alateen.org

Part of the Al-Anon Family Groups, this organization is for teens who must deal with an alcoholic family member, or who struggle with alcohol abuse themselves. Alateen groups are sponsored by Al-Anon members who help the group to stay on track. Alateen members come together to share experiences, strength, and hope with each other, discuss difficulties, learn effective ways to cope with problems, encourage one another, help each other understand the principles of the Al-Anon program, and learn how to use the Twelve Steps and Alateen's Twelve Traditions.

**American Beverage Institute (ABI)**
1090 Vermont Ave. NW, Ste. 800
Washington, DC 20005
(202) 463-7110
website: www.abionline.org

ABI is a restaurant industry trade organization that works to protect the consumption of alcoholic beverages in the restaurant setting. It unites the wine, beer, and spirits producers with distributors and on-premise retailers in this effort. It conducts research and education in an attempt to demonstrate that the vast majority of adults who drink alcohol outside of the home are responsible, law-abiding citizens. Its website includes fact sheets and news articles on various issues, such as drunk driving laws and alcohol taxes.

**American Society of Addiction Medicine (ASAM)**
4601 N. Park Ave., Upper Arcade #101
Chevy Chase, MD 20815
(301) 656-3920
e-mail: email@asam.org
website: www.asam.org

ASAM is the nation's addiction medicine specialty society dedicated to educating physicians and improving the treatment of individuals suffering from alcoholism and other addictions. In addition, the organization promotes research and prevention of addiction and works for the establishment of addiction medicine as a specialty recognized by the American Board of Medical Specialties. The organization publishes medical texts and a bimonthly newsletter.

**Campaign Against Drunk Driving (CADD)**
PO Box 62, Brighouse, West Yorkshire HD6 3YY
+44 (0)845 123-5541
e-mail: cadd@scard.org.uk
website: www.cadd.org.uk

CADD is a British organization dedicated to providing support to victims of drunk driving and to promoting stronger drunk driving laws, including a lower legal blood alcohol concentration level. Its website provides sources for drunk driving statistics in Great Britain.

**Center for Science in the Public Interest (CSPI)**
1875 Connecticut Ave. NW, Ste. 300
Washington, DC 20009
(202) 332-9110
e-mail: cspi@cspinet.org
website: www.cspinet.org

This advocacy organization promotes nutrition and health, food safety, alcohol policy, and sound science. It favors the implementation of public policies aimed at reducing alcohol-related problems, such as restricting alcohol advertising, increasing alcohol taxes, and reducing drunk driving.

**The Century Council**
2345 Crystal Dr., Ste. 910, Arlington, VA 22202
(202) 637-0077
website: www.centurycouncil.org

This organization, sponsored in part by the distilled spirits industry, supports programs and laws that help people enjoy alcohol responsibly. It encourages programs and organizations that curb underage drinking and generates public policy on binge drinking, underage drinking, and other alcohol-related laws. The council promotes responsible decision making about drinking and discourages all forms of irresponsible alcohol consumption through education, communications, research, law enforcement, and other programs. Its website offers fact sheets and other resources on drunk driving, underage drinking, and other alcohol-related problems.

**Distilled Spirits Council of the United States (DISCUS)**
1250 Eye St. NW, Ste. 400
Washington, DC 20005
(202) 628-3544
website: www.discus.org

DISCUS is the national trade association representing producers and marketers of distilled spirits in the United States. It seeks to ensure the responsible advertising and marketing of distilled spirits to adult consumers and to prevent such advertising and marketing from targeting individuals below the legal purchase age. It publishes fact sheets, news releases, and other documents.

**DWI Resource Center, Inc.**
PO Box 30514
Albuquerque, NM 87190
(888) 410-1084
e-mail: info@dwiresourcecenter.org
website: http://dwiresourcecenter.org

This organization's goal is to reduce the number of alcohol-related traffic fatalities through education, public awareness, prevention, and research. It serves as a central clearinghouse of driving-while-intoxicated (DWI) information and issues, providing community leaders with statistical information and analysis to assist them in creating localized plans to reduce DWI death and injury.

**International Center for Alcohol Policies (ICAP)**
1519 New Hampshire Ave. NW
Washington, DC 20036
(202) 986-1159
website: www.icap.org

This nonprofit organization is dedicated to helping reduce the abuse of alcohol worldwide and to promote understanding of the role of alcohol in society through dialogue and partnerships involving the beverage industry, the public health community, and others interested in alcohol policy. ICAP is supported by eleven major international alcoholic beverage companies.

**The Marin Institute**
24 Belvedere St., San Rafael, CA 94901
(415) 456-5692
website: www.marininstitute.org

The Marin Institute works to reduce alcohol problems by improving the physical and social environment to advance public health and safety. The institute promotes stricter alcohol policies—including higher taxes and a legal drinking age of twenty-one—in order to reduce alcohol-related problems. It publishes fact sheets and news alerts on alcohol policy, advertising, and other alcohol-related issues.

**Mothers Against Drunk Driving (MADD)**
511 E. John Carpenter Fwy., No. 700
Irving, TX 75062
(800) GET-MADD (438-6233)
e-mail: Information: info@madd.org • Victim's
Assistance: victims@madd.org
website: www.madd.org

MADD seeks to act as the voice of victims of drunk driving by speaking on their behalf to communities, businesses, and educational groups and by providing materials for use in medical facilities and health and driver education programs. MADD publishes the biannual *MADDvocate for Victims Magazine* and the newsletter *MADD in Action* as well as a variety of fact sheets, brochures, and other materials on drunk driving.

**National Commission Against Drunk Driving (NCADD)**
244 E. Fifty-Eighth St., 4th Fl.
New York, NY 10022
(212) 269-7797
e-mail: national@ncadd.org
website: www.ncadd.org

NCADD is a coalition of public and private organizations and others who work together to reduce impaired driving and its tragic consequences. Its website has a searchable database of abstracts of research studies that make an excellent research resource.

**National Institute on Alcohol Abuse and Alcoholism (NIAAA)**
5635 Fishers Ln., MSC 9304, Bethesda, MD 20892-9304
website: www.niaaa.nih.gov

The NIAAA is one of the eighteen institutes that compose the National Institutes of Health. The NIAAA provides leadership in the national effort to reduce alcohol-related problems such as drunk driving.

### National Youth Rights Association (NYRA)
1101 Fifteenth St. NW, Ste. 200
Washington, DC 20005
(202) 835-1719
website: www.youthrights.org

One of the many positions promoted by this organization for youth rights is a lowered drinking age. In addition to the voting age, curfews, and other issues, the NYRA supports policies and legislation that combat what it calls the "youth prohibitionist movement." Ample information about the history of the drinking age and numerous fact sheets appear on the group's website.

### Responsibility in DUI Laws, Inc. (RIDL)
PO Box 87053, Canton, MI 48188
e-mail: info@ridl.us
website www.ridl.us

RIDL believes current driving-under-the-influence (DUI) laws are too harsh and are aimed more at criminalizing and punishing responsible drinkers than curbing drunk driving. RIDL's mission is to educate the public and lawmakers about the misdirection of the current laws, take the steps necessary to get the current laws repealed, and to provide alternative suggestions for dealing with the problem of drunk driving.

### Secular Organizations for Sobriety (SOS)
4773 Hollywood Blvd.
Hollywood, CA 90027
(323) 666-4295
website: www.secularsobriety.org

SOS is a network of groups dedicated to helping individuals achieve and maintain sobriety. The organization believes that alcoholics can best recover by rationally choosing to make sobriety rather than alcohol a priority.

**Students Against Destructive Decisions (SADD)**
255 Main St., Marlborough, MA 01752
(877) SADD-INC (723-3462)
e-mail: info@sadd.org
website: www.sadd.org

Originally called Students Against Drunk Driving, SADD's mission later expanded to provide students with the best prevention and intervention tools possible to deal with the issues of underage drinking, other drug use, impaired driving, and other destructive decisions. SADD's website has statistics on teens and drunk driving along with information on how to form local SADD chapters.

**Substance Abuse and Mental Health
Services Administration (SAMHSA)
National Clearinghouse for Alcohol
and Drug Information (NCADI)**
PO Box 2345, Rockville, MD 20847-2345
(800) 729-6686
website: http://ncadi.samhsa.gov

SAMHSA is the division of the US Department of Health and Human Services that is responsible for improving the lives of those with or at risk for mental illness or substance addiction. Through the NCADI, SAMHSA provides the public with a wide variety of information on alcoholism and other addictions.

# BIBLIOGRAPHY

## Books

Dennis A. Bjorklund, *Drunk Driving Laws: Rules of the Road When Crossing State Lines*. 2nd ed. Iowa City, IA: Praetorian, 2008.

George W. Dowdall, *College Drinking: Reframing a Social Problem*. Westport, CT: Praeger, 2009.

David Edvin and Samuel Harald, eds., *Underage Drinking: Examining and Preventing Youth Use of Alcohol*. Hauppauge, NY: Nova Science, 2010.

Cecile A. Marczinski, Estee C. Grant, and Vincent J. Grant, eds., *Binge Drinking in Adolescents and College Students*. Hauppauge, NY: Nova Science, 2009.

Nathaniel P. Marquis, ed., *Preventing and Reducing Underage Drinking (Substance Abuse Assessment, Interventions and Treatment)*. Hauppauge, NY: Nova Science, 2009.

Marjana Martinic and Fiona Measham, eds., *Swimming with Crocodiles: The Culture of Extreme Drinking*. New York: Routledge, 2008.

Garrett Peck, *The Prohibition Hangover: Alcohol in America from Demon Rum to Cult Cabernet*. Piscataway, NJ: Rutgers University Press, 2009.

## Periodicals and Internet Sources

Stephenson Billings, "Should the Legal Drinking Age Be Raised to 25 to Eliminate Deadly College Partying?," Christwire.org, October 24, 2010. http://christwire.org/2010/10/should-the -legal-drinking-age-be-raised-to-25-to-eliminate-deadly-college -partying.

*Dallas Morning News*, "Parents Fail Other Parents in Curbing Teen Drinking," October 18, 2010. www.dallasnews.com/opinion /editorials/20101018-Editorial-Parents-fail-other-parents-1772 .ece.

Abigail Field, "The Case Against Banning Four Loko," DailyFinance, November 15, 2010. www.dailyfinance.com/2010/11/15/the -case-against-banning-four-loko/.

Jeff Gaither, "Evils of Underage Drinking Exaggerated," *University Wire*, April 11, 2007. www.highbeam.com/doc/1P1-137609724 .html.

*Gloucester (MA) Times*, "Four Loko Drink Ban Misses the Mark Fighting Alcohol Abuse," November 18, 2010. www.glouces tertimes.com/opinion/x117336651/Editorial-Four-Loko-drink -ban-misses-the-mark-fighting-alcohol-abuse.

*Kentucky Kernel* (University of Kentucky), "Drinking Age Limit Protects Students, Should Remain 21," November 15, 2009. http://kykernel.com/2009/11/15/drinking-age-limit-protects -students-should-remain-21.

*Los Angeles Times*, "Flash! Facebook Causes Teen Drinking (Until You Read the Fine Print)," August 25, 2011. http://opinion.lat imes.com/opinionla/2011/08/flash-facebook-causes-teen-drink ing-until-you-read-the-fine-print.html.

National Center on Addiction and Substance Abuse at Columbia University, "National Survey of American Attitudes on Substance Abuse XVI: Teens and Parents," 2011. www.casaco lumbia.org/upload/2011/20110824teensurveyreport.pdf.

Toben F. Nelson and Traci L. Toomey, "Drinking Age of 21 Saves Lives," CNN.com, September 28, 2009. http://articles.cnn .com/2009-09-29/us/nelson.retain.drinking.age_1_amethyst -initiative-drinking-age-binge-drink?_s=PM:US.

Glenn Harlan Reynolds, "Old Enough to Fight, Old Enough to Drink," *Wall Street Journal*, April 13, 2011. http://online.wsj .com/article/SB10001424052748704641604576255161172364 474.html.

*Washington Post*, "A Lower Drinking Age?," July 12, 2009. www .washingtonpost.com/wp-dyn/content/arctile/2009/07/11 /AR2009071102337.html.

## Websites

**Amethyst Initiative (www.amethystinitiative.org).** View the list of college and university chancellors and presidents who have signed the Amethyst Initiative, which seeks to lower the drinking age to eighteen to reduce the problem of binge drinking on campuses.

**Choose Responsibility (www.chooseresponsibility.org).** This organization promotes lowering the drinking age to eighteen. It contains useful resources for parents, educators, and students.

**College Drinking Prevention (www.collegedrinkingprevention. gov).** This site, maintained by the National Institute on Alcohol Abuse and Alcoholism (NIAAA), focuses on the problem of drinking in college and explores various solutions.

**The Cool Spot: Alcohol, Peer Pressure, Teenage Underage Drinking (www.thecoolspot.gov)** .This site, sponsored by multiple government departments, helps teens resist peer pressure to drink and gives them information about the health risks of underage drinking.

**Don't Let Minors Drink (www.dontletminorsdrink.com).** This site, sponsored by the Pennsylvania Liquor Control Board, contains a wealth of resources for fighting the problem of underage drinking. The site contains useful reports and studies and ideas for how students can reduce underage drinking at their schools.

**Preventing Adolescent Binge Drinking (www.youthbingedrinking. org).** This site seeks to prevent teenage binge drinking by helping teens understand the dangers and consequences of binge drinking.

**Underage Drinking Enforcement Training Center (www.udetc .org).** This program was established by the Office of Juvenile Justice and Delinquency Prevention (within the US Department of Justice). Its goal is to build leadership capacity and increase the effectiveness of states and local communities in their efforts to enforce underage drinking laws, prevent underage drinking, and eliminate the devastating consequences associated with alcohol use by underage youth.

**We Don't Serve Teens (www.dontserveteens.gov).** This site is maintained by the Federal Trade Commission and contains useful information about underage drinking laws and penalties by state.

National Institute on Drug
Abuse (NIDA), 20, 33
National Institutes of Health,
20
National Minimum Drinking
Age Act (1984), 19, 48
National Survey on Drug Use
and Health, 52
*New York Times* (newspaper),
21, 81
NHTSA (National
Highway Traffic Safety
Administration), 27, 80
*Nicomachean Ethics*
(Aristotle), 83
NIDA (National Institute on
Drug Abuse), 20, 33

O'Connor, Mary, 68, 71
Opinion polls. *See* Surveys

Parents
should let teens drink at
home, 60–65
should not let teens drink at
home, 66–71
survey of, 65
Phusion Projects, 75
Polls. *See* Surveys
Pregnancy, unplanned, 16
Presidential Commission on
Drunk Driving, 43
Prevention/prevention
programs, 27–28
through alcohol education
classes, 91–94

Primack, Brian, 68, 70
Prohibition, 31–33, 45, 54
*Psychology of Addictive
Behaviors*, 57

Rangan, Cyrus, 5
Rasul, Jawaid W., 49
Rothbard, Murray, 34–35

SAMHSA (Substance Abuse
and Mental Health Services
Administration), 10, 62
Schelenz, Robyn, 72
Schumer, Charles, 80
Scribner, Richard A., 47–48,
49
Sexual behavior, risky, role of
alcohol in, 16–17
Sexually transmitted diseases
(STDs), 16
Single-sex dormitories, can
prevent underage drinking,
82–86
*St. Petersburg Times*
(newspaper), 81
Substance Abuse and
Mental Health Services
Administration (SAMHSA),
10, 62
Suicides
attributable to alcohol, 16
percentage of teen deaths due
to, *40*
Sullum, Jacob, 77
Surveys
on alcohol use among high
school seniors, 48

# PICTURE CREDITS